Semantic Media

"Nothing should be named lest by so doing we change it."

The Waves, Virginia Woolf

"The perfect search engine should understand exactly what you mean."

Amit Singhal, former Senior Vice President of Search, Google

Semantic Media

Mapping Meaning on the Internet

Andrew Iliadis

polity

First published in 2023 by Polity Press

Polity Press
65 Bridge Street
Cambridge CB2 1UR, UK

Polity Press
111 River Street
Hoboken, NJ 07030, USA

ISBN-13: 978-1-5095-4257-4
ISBN-13: 978-1-5095-4258-1(pb)

A catalogue record for this book is available from the British Library.

Library of Congress Control Number: 2022938560

Typeset in 11 on 13 pt Sabon
by Fakenham Prepress Solutions, Fakenham, Norfolk NR21 8NL
Printed and bound in the UK by CPI Group (UK) Ltd, Croydon

For further information on Polity, visit our website:
politybooks.com

Contents

Figures and Tables

Figures

Tables

Acknowledgments

Writing this book would not have been possible without the people who, directly or indirectly, supported it along the way. I'd like to thank all the wonderful mentors, teachers, students, colleagues, and friends that I have had the good fortune of working with and learning from over the last several years, before and after the start of my position at Temple University. My home in Temple's Department of Media Studies and Production, within the Klein College of Media and Communication, has been a happy one.

The students at Temple have been outstanding. I want to thank those who participated in my Introduction to Media Theory, Technology and Culture, and Information and Society undergraduate classes and those in my Communication Research Methods and Social Media Analytics graduate classes. Our conversations and projects have helped me reflect on my research practices and approaches to pedagogy, and I have learned a lot from our shared experiences. I have also benefited from working with several fantastic student research assistants, including Wesley Stevens, Christiana Dillard, Aiden Kosciesza, and Sezgi Kavakli.

I'm grateful to be working in an environment that fosters collaboration and mentorship among colleagues. I'd particularly like to thank my colleagues in the department who have made research at Temple a joy. My thanks to Geoffrey Baym, Amy Caples, Alice Castellini, Sherri Hope Culver, Jan Fernback, Matt Fine, Paul Gluck, Tom Jacobson, Peter Jaroff, Jack Klotz, Lauren Kogen, Joseph Kraus, Marc Lamont Hill, Matthew Lombard, Larisa Mann, Nancy Morris, Patrick Murphy, Wazhmah Osman, Hector Postigo, Clemencia Rodríguez, Adrienne Shaw, Betsy Leebron Tutelman, Barry Vacker, Kristine Weatherston, and Laura Zaylea.

As part of our college, I've had the good fortune of working on research and service with colleagues in other Klein departments over the last few years. I'd also like to give special thanks to Deborah Cai, Erin Coyle, Brian Creech, Fabienne Darling-Wolf, Edward Fink, Scott Gratson, Bruce Hardy, Don Heller, Lance Holbert, Tricia Jones, Carolyn Kitch, Magda Konieczna, Heather LaMarre, David Mindich, Logan Molyneux, Kathy Mueller, Devon Powers, Dana Saewitz, Soomin Seo, Meghnaa Tallapragada, Lori Tharps, Karen Turner, and Andrea Wenzel. Extra special thanks to our Dean at Klein, David Boardman, who has shown extraordinary leadership during my time at Temple.

This book would not have been possible without a Sabbatical Award and Grant-in-Aid Award from Temple. Both provided me with the time and resources to complete the manuscript.

I thank Neal Thomas, Ryan Shaw, Patrick Golden, Melanie Feinberg, and the Organization Research Group at the University of North Carolina at Chapel Hill. They provided constructive feedback on a draft of the manuscript. Heather Ford (School of Communication, University of Technology, Sydney) aided my thinking throughout the project and provided inspiration for many of its ideas, leading to new and exciting research projects. Amelia Acker (School of Information, University of Texas at Austin) also read a draft and helped improve the book; she has been a great writing partner, collaborator, and friend. Isabel Pedersen (Faculty of Social Science and Humanities, Ontario Tech University) has been an extraordinary mentor and confidant; I'm fortunate to continue collaborating with Isabel and everyone at Ontario Tech's Decimal Lab and the Digital Life Institute.

The team at Polity did an incredible job helping me complete this book, from pitch to publication. Thanks to Mary Savigar, Stephanie Homer, Ellen MacDonald-Kramer, Ian Tuttle, and the anonymous reviewers who provided feedback.

I wanted to write a book that would be interesting for a non-specialist audience. I'm not sure if the book succeeds in this respect—if it does, it is thanks to those who have helped me rethink media scholarship; any shortcomings can be attributed solely to me.

Some of the research in this book has appeared in another form in my academic articles. I recognize these previous works, which include the following: "Algorithms, ontology, and social progress," *Global Media and Communication* (2018), "The Tower of Babel problem: Making data make sense with basic formal ontology," *Online Information Review* (2019), and "The seer and the seen: Surveying Palantir's surveillance platform," *The Information Society* (2022), and also as-yet-unpublished manuscripts titled "One schema to rule them all: How Schema.org models the world of search" and "Fabricating facts: A semantic network analysis of the Wikidata ontology."

I wrote parts of this book in Canada, on Manitoulin Island. Special thanks to Nick, Amanda, and Charlie for hosting me.

Lastly, to my parents, Cathy and Jim, my brother Michael, Lindsay, Edward, my aunts, uncles, and cousins—nothing has enriched my life more than our big, happy family. I dedicate this book to the memories of my grandparents.

Andrew Iliadis, Philadelphia, 2022

Introduction

Where do you usually look when you need to quickly find a piece of information? People who can afford them tend to use their smartphones or laptops to browse their preferred social media platforms to catch up on the day's news (Pew Research Center, 2021). But what about when you casually want to find an answer to a specific question, like when a revolutionary figure was born, or when you want to look up a common fact (like the official capital of Canada)? Maybe you're searching for a vegan recipe or the director of a documentary. Or perhaps you're looking up the alma mater of a politician or an exciting book that you heard about but whose title currently escapes you.

No matter what fact you look for, our technologies can quickly provide you with an answer without hassle. If you're like most people with an internet connection and a computer, you will type (or speak) your query into a search engine (or virtual assistant) to get the answer.[1] Depending on your service, the device will neatly display your solution in panels, menus, and labels directly in the search results (or the device will read aloud to you). Most of the time, your search ends right there with the initial results without requiring you to seek any additional items.

You usually don't have to follow any links or visit other sites because the information and facts are already neatly presented.

According to some controversial search engine studies, searches like this done today are considered "zero-click"—people find what they need with a single search and do not need to navigate to other sources (Fishkin, 2019, 2021; Ferguson, 2021; Sullivan, 2021). The ability to conduct zero-click searches might seem helpful to many of us, efficient even. Some of us probably wouldn't think twice about it, grateful to receive our information and go about our day.

Yet, when pressed, problems quickly arise. What if someone asked you from where the resulting facts (displayed or spoken) came? Could you identify a source or give a correct answer? "Google" or "Wikipedia" would likely be common responses. "Alexa" or "Siri" might be other replies. These would be excellent but vague guesses, and they would miss some insidious new features of internet-based media technologies. Alternatively, I might use a spatial image and ask you exactly *where* these facts were stored (in your phone, on a website, search engine, etc.) and how your chosen application found them. More pointedly, what if I asked you about the *verifiability* of the answer you received? How would you know if the solution you saw in the results was accurate? What criteria would you use to determine that accuracy?

More each day, media technologies provide facts in our searches instead of leading us to different sources. Search engines, applications, platforms, and virtual assistants are now in the business of articulating information for us in answer to our questions.[2] Our searches increasingly do not lead to other sources (ranked lists of Google search results, Wikipedia pages, etc.) but end with answers that appear to be provided by the companies that own the products we are using. These processes suggest that we are in a relatively new media era. This era began about a decade ago when companies started to focus on products that try to guess our *intentions* and what we are trying to know by offering direct answers to queries based on *context*. Such products began to also provide mechanisms for *actions* based on our searches (buying tickets, scheduling an appointment, etc.), becoming more central in our daily lives (Kofler et al., 2016). Part of this shift is due to the changing nature of our search behaviors. Yet, a large part comes from the fact that internet companies attempt to position themselves as internet users' "one-stop-shop" location for obtaining information, thus decreasing our need for browsing.

This book is about what I refer to as *semantic media*, which I describe as media technologies that orchestrate and directly convey facts, answers, meanings, and "knowledge" about things directly in media products, rather than leading people to other sources.[3] The book describes the often-invisible ways (to the non-specialist) that internet companies are now actively involved in constructing information about the world. The book is about how organizations like Apple, Google, Facebook, Amazon, and Microsoft are in the business of creating and storing facts to be served up to users in new and emerging media products and what this might mean for knowledge in the future. It will look at how design decisions *bake* these facts into the apps and platforms people use daily while focusing on the infrastructures dedicated to orchestrating and presenting this information. The goal is to understand the technologies that will drive social and political outcomes when large internet companies become a primary conduit through which people directly acquire an understanding of facts about the world. But perhaps a more concrete example will help.

Macedonia

My family is Macedonian, and my parents have always told me that the name of the mountainous village from which my family emigrated (before I was born) is named Armensko, located in what is today known as northern Greece. Almost all my family is from the region; my father was born there, including my grandparents on both sides. Half my family still lives there. When large portions of the family immigrated to Toronto, they brought the culture and language with them. In Toronto, I grew up speaking Macedonian, attending Macedonian folk dancing lessons, and attending Macedonian weddings and social events.

When I use Google to search for "Armensko" on my laptop, the response I receive in the panels is for Armenia (Google thinks I've made a typo). If I search instead for "Armensko, Greece," the results this time return a panel (Google calls these *knowledge panels*) for a village called Alona, including a Google Map image showing a geographic location identical to what I know of as Armensko. Also included are Wikipedia details (which Google has orchestrated) for the Alona entry, along with bits of information like its municipality, elevation, etc. I examine the images displayed directly in the knowledge panel where I see a photograph (probably one from the Wikipedia entry). The graphic is a small black and white photo of the village I recognize, dated 1917 (figure 0.1). The name printed on the photo reads "Armensko" (the name of my family's village) and not "Alona" (the official name returned in the Google results).

On the one hand, there's an apparent reason that Google's panels show information for a village called "Alona" instead of "Armensko." "Alona" is the official Greek name of the location, and "Armensko" is its Macedonian name. Like similar geographical naming disputes, there is a long and complex history of war, migration, and identity tied to this tiny mountainous village in the Balkans.

The region that the village sits in is part of the Balkan Peninsula and a historically contested transnational space called "Macedonia" that has roots in antiquity and that

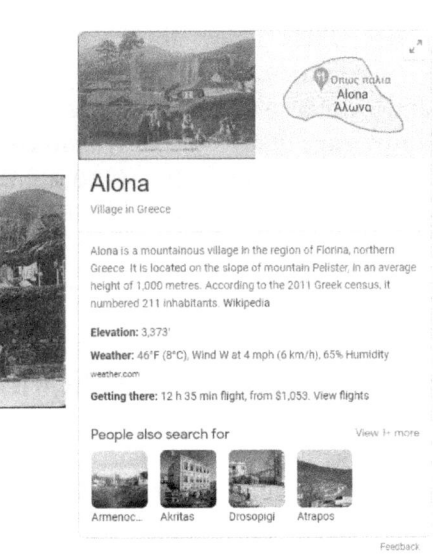

Alona
Village in Greece

Alona is a mountainous village in the region of Florina, northern Greece. It is located on the slope of mountain Pelister, in an average height of 1,000 metres. According to the 2011 Greek census, it numbered 211 inhabitants. Wikipedia

Elevation: 3,373'

Weather: 46°F (8°C), Wind W at 4 mph (6 km/h), 65% Humidity
weather.com

Getting there: 12 h 35 min flight, from $1,053. View flights

People also search for   View 1+ more

Armenoc...   Akritas   Drosopigi   Atrapos

Feedback

Figure 0.1: Knowledge panel for Armensko
Source: WikimediaCommons

today contains parts of Serbia, Kosovo, Albania, and Bulgaria, all of North Macedonia, and a large portion of northern Greece. Borders in the region shifted because of the Balkan Wars, the decline of the Ottoman Empire, and the dissolution of Yugoslavia, and Slavic Macedonians did not achieve statehood until 1991 (the country now called North Macedonia). The Macedonian area of what is now northern Greece is where Slavic Macedonians like my family live, yet many fled due to compelled emigration and forced renaming of towns and family names after the Greek Civil War. Greece and North Macedonia have both laid claim to the term "Macedonia" (one Greek, the other Slavic) since 1991, and this has resulted in over 30 years of tension and instability in the region.

No wonder Google has a hard time with this query about a Macedonian village; how is Google's knowledge panel expected to capture these meaningful nuances? Yet, Google attempts to provide an answer in the knowledge panel when asked about the location of Armensko by giving information for Armenia (completely incorrect) and Alona (somewhat correct). According to Google's knowledge panel, Slavic Armensko may never have existed, which is strange to me. Odd, considering that I grew up visiting a place people told me was called Armensko while speaking Macedonian with residents, many of whom still live there.[4]

Where Trees Stand in Water

Now, suppose I search for a larger city like Toronto. In this case, Google's knowledge panel contains much more information, including an official summary that Google does not appear to take from Wikipedia. Instead, it seems as though Google wrote it (the description is authoritatively marked "—Google" at the end). There is information presented from Weather.com, population information from the United Nations, links to Toronto's current mayor, area codes, universities, etc. Though Toronto's municipal website foregrounds land acknowledgments in the Accessibility & Human Rights section, the Google knowledge panel neglects to mention that Toronto is on indigenous land, including that of the Mississaugas of the Credit, the Anishnabeg, the Chippewa, the Haudenosaunee, and the Wendat peoples. Like the Alona/Armensko example, the knowledge panel contains what Google thinks is the most relevant information about Toronto, rather than any indigenous information about *Tkaronto*, the original name that Aboriginal and Indigenous peoples use, which means something to the effect of "where the trees stand in the water" (Recollet & Johnson, 2019).

Some impatient people might argue that it makes sense that Google should present searchers with facts and information about Alona in its knowledge panels and not Armensko. Or that it should be acceptable that

Google's knowledge panel for Toronto does not mention Tkaronto or Indigenous land. Their hasty argument might be that most people who use the knowledge panel are looking for quick and contemporary information like the weather, people in leadership, and a description of the geography. Yet, one can also argue that focusing only on such details elides the complex histories and identities that make people and locations what they are. This type of decision is an example of the tradeoffs that today's media companies are willing to make. Companies like Google are interested in providing quick facts and answers in their "intuitive" search results, providing the most "relevant" facts to most users. Yet, in doing so, such companies imagine a type of ideal proxy customer that does not exist (Mulvin, 2021).

Such results tell us something interesting about the *temporality* of the factual content that media technology companies think they should provide (always show content that applies to the "here and now").[5] They also tell us something about their approach to *verifying* information (seldom are references provided). For example, it is not clear that people will always want only a snapshot of the current and "official" facts about a geographic location instead of a deeper cultural understanding. As of this writing, search engines also do not always build into their search products things like provenance information (Hartig, 2009) concerning where data come from or digital heritage information (Kremers, 2020) about cultural history. In terms of reference, the most people can hope for are tiny blue links, but knowledge panels do not always include these.

Similarly, virtual assistants like Siri and Alexa do not usually inform users about the history of information or the sourcing and verifiability of facts that they retrieve. Sometimes we are lucky if they cite Wikipedia. These practices omit and foreclose what Acker (2015) has called the *hermeneutics* of data—how we might go about interpreting data that inform the facts that we receive.

The Power to Name

Media technology companies have incredible power to name.[6] Researchers such as Ford and Graham (2016a, 2016b) have critically addressed the semantic power that companies like Google have in naming, managing, and establishing popular understandings of places. "Semantics" should be understood here broadly as to how people linguistically and logically create meaning for words, sentences, and texts. Journalists have covered Ford and Graham's work in *The Washington Post* in an article titled "You probably haven't even noticed Google's sketchy quest to control the world's knowledge" (Dewey, 2016). The report examines how Google now attempts to answer controversial questions like "What is the capital of Israel?" or mundane queries like "What is D.C.'s best restaurant?" Google's knowledge panels are supposed to bring this information directly to you in the form of facts, and these facts often include contested and controversial statements. Ford and Graham's work on the status of contested cities and locations (for example, Jerusalem or Taiwan) and how Google represents them is evidence of Google's power to make important decisions about how we understand facts and the meanings that are associated with those places (Graham, 2015).

Journalists at other newspapers also note the immense control that media technology companies have in presenting facts. In 2019, *The Wall Street Journal* published an article titled "How Google interferes with its search algorithms and changes your results" (Grind et al., 2019). The article describes the increasing importance of things like knowledge panels, which many people now rely on when looking up facts. The authors state that "Google engineers regularly make behind-the-scenes adjustments to other information the company is increasingly layering on top of its basic search results" and that these often include "boxes called 'knowledge panels.'" The reporting documents that specific facts and words appear on internal blocklists that "affect the results in organic search and Google News, as well as other search products, such as Web answers and knowledge panels." There is a significant amount of power that Google has regarding information articulated in these knowledge panels.

Let's Take a Trip

Media technology companies have the power to name and express facts and definitions about things, but they also now can organize these facts in interactive ways beyond static knowledge panels. Companies display facts in orchestrated *carousels* (movable tracks where people can cycle through results) and *featured boxes* (containing lists with dropdown menus). Like the knowledge panels described above, carousels and featured boxes often rely on a *taxonomy* (an organized set of definitions and classifications) created by the media company. These taxonomies can be about anything: German actors, aid organizations, dictators, biological information, tourist recommendations, etc. Who is it that is making these categories? How do media companies decide what pieces of information to include in them?

Let's switch to a different search engine. If I search Bing for "Things to do in Philadelphia," Microsoft will produce many buttons and dropdown menus with what Microsoft thinks are pertinent information categories (figure 0.2a). These include things like "Things to do," "Events," "What to Eat," etc., which then break down into topic areas like "Architecture," "Outdoors," "Museums," etc. The categories appear to be coming from Microsoft, as there is no discernible information about their creation. Different sites display their data as one browses these categories, including TripAdvisor, Wikipedia, etc. Yet, all this orchestrated information remains on Bing—as I click and browse, I never have to leave Bing's page. It's

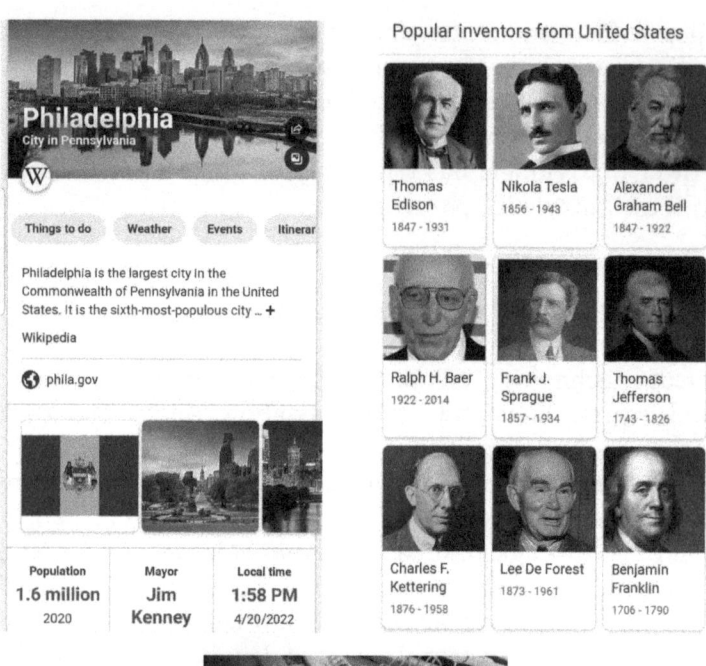

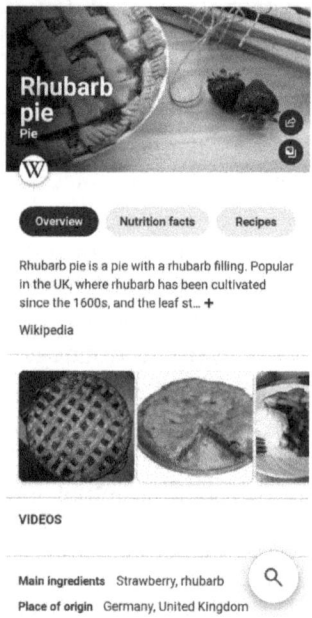

Figure 0.2: Bing results showing carousels, featured boxes, and knowledge panels

almost as if Bing has a micro-website for every topic, as it quickly retrieves information and organizes it for me using Bing's proprietary algorithms and taxonomy. Bing quickly provides a full day's worth of activities for me, and I didn't even visit another website. This decrease in browsing has a negative effect on local websites and apps. Furthermore, such results often contain significant sociocultural biases. If I ask for a list of "American inventors," the resulting featured box labeled "Popular inventors from United States" is made up entirely of men (figure 0.2b).

Internet-based media technology companies today want one thing: to allow you to do everything (look up facts, take specific actions, etc.) all directly on their media products. This process might seem innocuous at first. Who wouldn't want helpful details about prices and store opening hours quickly made available? Yet, as we shall see, there are deeper problems associated with knowledge representation and information retrieval that this book will explain. How do Google and Microsoft decide what information to produce about events, things, people, and locations in their media products like knowledge panels and virtual assistants? Some data appear to be authoritative and come directly from the companies, while some appear from different sources (and attribution is not always discernible). The knowledge panels answer a searcher's query regardless of the data source. Media companies orchestrate these facts somehow. This book is about the technologies that enable this type of information to be discoverable on knowledge panels, virtual assistants, platforms, and beyond.

Almost Everyone

The results concerning who receives a knowledge panel, what gets included, and where linked resources lead vary drastically. If I search for "Turkish coffee" or recipes for "Rhubarb pie," Google or Bing will provide a knowledge panel that lists the main ingredients (figure 0.2c). Each has navigable links back to Google or Bing knowledge panels for every item (it's a loop that keeps you on their product). Some information in the description is from Wikipedia, while on other occasions, it is not. Google also offers a "Feedback" button in the knowledge panel where I can correct specific sections, such as if the calories are off or the recipe is incorrect. This feedback goes to Google, and the company then makes some determinations about editing the knowledge panel. But not all recipes receive a knowledge panel—currently, there is no knowledge panel for the popular Ethiopian dish *kitfo*, for example. Some recipes appear in Google's rich results and dropdown menus, lifted from things like personal websites. People will see these recipes and never have to visit the sites that originally posted the material.

On Facebook, if I search for Milo Yiannopoulos (the extreme rightwing media personality), I receive a knowledge panel about him, who he is, etc. (unlike some results on Alexa and Google, which do not indicate a source, Facebook notes this information is from Wikipedia). Like Google, Facebook also offers the opportunity to provide feedback by including an "Is this information accurate?" button. Yet, who receives a knowledge panel on Facebook (as with Google) seems somewhat random. For example, currently, Joseph Stalin has a knowledge panel, while Che Guevara does not. John Schnatter (the founder of Papa John's pizzas) has a knowledge panel. But there is no knowledge panel for Sir Lady Java (the activist and entertainer), who helped start the transgender rights movement in the United States in the 1960s.

As Noble (2018) shows in her essential book *Algorithms of oppression: How search engines reinforce racism*, many large platform companies offer results that are culturally, racially, and sexually biased in their oversimplification of representation:

> What we find in search engines about people and culture is important. They oversimplify complex phenomena. They

obscure any struggle over understanding, and they can mask history. Search results can reframe our thinking and deny us the ability to engage deeply with essential information and knowledge we need, knowledge that has traditionally been learned through teachers, books, history, and experience.

Noble's book clarifies how search results from large platform companies can often show significant racial bias in autocomplete term suggestions as users type search queries, what images display in search results, and how links are ranked. She describes how search "does not merely present pages but structures knowledge, and the results retrieved in a commercial search engine create their particular material reality." A robust critical tradition of search engine studies focuses on these themes. Halavais' (2008/2017) *Search engine society* laid the groundwork for critically reflecting on the habits of search engine users and the search results of major internet platforms, while Vaidhyanathan's (2011) *The Googlization of everything* provided a significant political economy perspective on search companies like Google and their knowledge monopoly. As technology evolves, there are new opportunities to bring such sustained critiques to bear on the political economy of today's corporate knowledge infrastructures, as Haider and Sundin (2019) have in their comprehensive work on the histories and new directions of search engines and search studies.[7]

A Shift in Search

One thing is clear: the media we use when searching for facts has changed. Whether the information comes from external or internal sources, platforms build mechanisms to present facts and answers about our world into their media products. They answer questions about everything from cities and people to ingredients and pies, which has enormous implications for how media function now and in the future. We already worry about companies like Google acting as gatekeepers to information regarding their ability to rank and link to sites (privileging some websites higher in the rankings) or Wikipedia containing uneven coverage in its content. We must also worry about how these companies directly convey facts in media products. Companies organize and manipulate this presentation of facts; the data is sometimes overtly biased, of unknown origin, and has social and political consequences.[8]

Search results have changed drastically since the days of Ask Jeeves, an early and popular search engine from the 1990s built for answering natural language questions (Ask Jeeves was a market competitor before the rise and domination of Google). Since roughly 2012, Google has similarly focused on deepening its search responses to answer questions about people, places, and things to create something like a "Star Trek computer" (Ingraham, 2012). Yet, it was not long before journalists started noticing less-than-stellar responses in the curated answers—including, for example, results offering creationist (religious) accounts of the dinosaurs and their extinction (Jacoby, 2016).

Errors aside, 2012 represented a significant change in how large media technology companies conceptualized information search and retrieval. They began to focus on framing inquiry in terms of the logical *concepts of things* (e.g., identifying people, places, entities) based on taxonomies rather than only the algorithmic *sorting of strings* (e.g., ranked lists of blue links) based on keyword similarity. The difference is between previously conceptualizing a search for a city like Philadelphia as a search for only the *word* "Philadelphia" (which would return websites that have the word "Philadelphia" on them) versus conceptualizing the inquiry as being for the *place* called "Philadelphia" (which would return information about the actual city). The second chapter provides a closer look at this transformational change in search.

Such a focus on concepts of things continues, particularly in the current increased climate of misinformation, the COVID-19 pandemic, and conspiracy theories. In 2018, in part as a response to misinformation from the 2016 US presidential election and the lies of former US President Donald Trump, Google announced that they would "spend $300 million over the next three years to help combat the spread of misinformation online and help journalism outlets" (Shaban, 2018). Knowledge graphs (large databases of facts) would play a crucial part in this project. Later the following year, Google released a white paper titled "How Google fights disinformation." The report describes how the company is attempting to give users more context in searches, including through their knowledge and information panels that provide "high-level facts about a person or issue" and make it "easier to discover the work of fact-checkers on Google." The company explains that they will include these facts in results to provide "users with contextual information from trusted sources to help them be more informed consumers of content on the platform" (Google, 2019).

Companies like Google are now engaged in the increasing semanticization of digital domains. They interpret, label, organize, and provide facts, acting as intermediaries between people and information. Such practices are evident with COVID-19, where search engines relay information in knowledge panels, such as statistics about current cases and deaths. Companies provide these statistics with accompanying charts and maps, and the data in this context typically reference sources such as Our World in Data or *The New York Times*. Google results for COVID-19 include a link labeled "About this data," which, when clicked, leads to a page that states that "Data comes from Wikipedia, government health ministries, *The New York Times*, and other authoritative sources, as attributed." This information is beneficial, and one can understand why it may be necessary to include it in semantically enriched search results.

There are other contexts where the decision to enhance information semantically is questionable. On the Bing results page for the search term "Trump," the knowledge panel does not include information about the conspiracy theory to reverse the 2020 election outcome or any negative information about the former president. Instead, it bizarrely lists quotes from Trump, such as "Sometimes by losing a battle you find a new way to win the war." The quote has no immediately discernible reference around it, yet it leads to BrainyQuote.com. The knowledge panel also lists facts, including that Trump has 18 golf courses, hosted *The Apprentice*, owns a private conglomerate comprised of 500 companies, and generated at least $59 million by licensing his name. None of these facts have easily identifiable sources. Instead, the addresses to the sources are unnumbered and grouped at the bottom, and there is no way to tell which link pairs with which fact. Users must click on the fact to see where it leads. The first one about golf courses links to a Medium article. Medium is a publishing site where it is "possible for anyone to blog and be seen" (Owen, 2019). When I search for the author's name (could they be a reputable journalist?), not much comes up except the author's other Medium posts, including two titled "How to disguise extra-terrestrials as humanoids" and "Is Big Foot real or fake?" The fact about *The Apprentice* leads to a History.com article, and the fact about Trump's company links to Encyclopædia Britannica. The panel contains information about Trump's movies and shows. Nowhere does the panel say anything about Trump's numerous conspiracy theories, lies, or disinformation about any matter, even though these are central to understanding who Trump is today.

Can You Trust a Knowledge Panel?

Google and other companies are attempting to combat misinformation with knowledge panels, but they also contain many errors. These errors do not seem to faze people, who by and large seem to trust knowledge panels. A recent search engine survey asked people if they trust the type of organic results that appear in Google searches. The results showed 51% of respondents "indicated that they 'very frequently' or 'often' make important life decisions based on Google information" and that "95% of respondents across all age groups find the Knowledge Panel results to be at least 'trustworthy'" (Ray, 2020)—an astonishingly high number. These results are fascinating, given reported errors with the technology, such as mixing up names, dates, descriptions, and what the panel ignores or omits.

For example, *The New York Times* once cheerfully documented Google and Microsoft's vision of "a future where search pages know what you mean, display exactly the information you want with one click and even perform tasks for you" (Pogue, 2012). Yet, a few years later, Rachel Abrams, a reporter at the same paper, went viral when she explained how she fought for a week trying to convince Google's Knowledge Graph to fix the panel about her to show that she wasn't, in fact, deceased (Abrams, 2017). What ended up happening was that the knowledge graph confused Rachel Abrams' picture with information about another Rachel Abrams, the (at the time) recently deceased writer. The name of Google's data graph product in which the Abrams error occurred, Knowledge Graph, has caught on and is now used when describing similar technologies at other companies across industries.

There are countless examples of missing or incorrect information and sociocultural biases in these knowledge panels. For example, a content strategist on Twitter, Michael Andrews, found that a search for "Kafka" returned knowledge panel results describing the software called Apache Kafka. Google did not return knowledge panel results for the famous Czech writer from whom the software takes its name (a fittingly Kafkaesque scenario). The researcher Pip Thornton (2017, 2018) has found that Google's search and advertising monetize language in regular search results, creating a semantic mismatch between the words you put into the search engine and the words that appear in the results. For example, if you search for "cloud," all the results will relate to cloud technology, even if you intended to search for the clouds in the sky or in Wordsworth's "I wandered lonely as a cloud" poem. A search for the word "sky" returned a knowledge panel for the British telecoms company with the same name. Google is slowly unrolling disambiguation options for knowledge panels, so this does not continue to occur, but many of these sociocultural biases remain.

After casually searching for content, industry professionals like Aaron Bradley (a knowledge graph strategist at Electronic Arts) have shared errors in knowledge panels on Twitter. Sometimes this will be in the form of mixing up the photo versus the description or when two different entities share the same name. Some examples: Elijah Wood is the name of an actor and a drummer; the title *Landline* is the name of a comedy and a porn movie; Batman is a place in Turkey and a fictional character; Don Cherry is the name of a jazz trumpeter and the (former, disgraced) hockey commentator—all of these have had information mixed up in knowledge panels at some point.

It does not take much imagination to see how these mistakes can negatively affect people. A viral tweet by the Native American TV writer and media company founder, Lucas Brown Eyes, noted that Google knowledge panels no longer retrieve anything related to Indigenous people when searching for names like "Dakota," "Pontiac," and "Chinook." The data scientist Takamitsu Tanaka once asked Google about wars in Europe since World War II, and the reply in the panel was: "Since the end of World War II, no wars have been fought in Europe" (this is false). The AI researcher Jiahao Chen once shared that Google Scholar wanted to consolidate the accounts of his and another researcher with the same name (the service is notorious for its referencing mistakes and restrictions;

Harzing, 2018). My acquaintance, the DJ and producer Ciel, had her music mixed up in the knowledge panel with music by a band with the same name. Accuracy, it seems, does not always come first with these tools.

Companies also copy content in these rich results. Some people have their images in their panels—Google previously patented retrieving social media photos via facial recognition to share in search results in 2010. As discussed above, you can read recipes in dropdown menus without ever visiting someone's site. A marketing specialist once pointed out this frustrating feature to a Google employee on Twitter. The employee asked for scraper websites to be reported (websites that copy content). The specialist had found a scraper site that was scraping content *about scraper sites* (what they are, etc.) from Wikipedia, and the joke was that the website doing the scraping was *Google*. Google has been increasing the amount of its content in results, but much is from other sources. According to previous Google leadership, such tradeoffs seem acceptable when finding facts. When asked about Knowledge Graph, Amit Singhal, a former Senior Vice President of Search at Google, answered that search engines are like "an amazing Swiss Army Knife. It's great, but sometimes you need to open a wine bottle. Some genius added that to the knife. That's awesome. That's how we think of the Knowledge Graph. Sometimes you only need an answer" (Schwartz, 2014).

Errors like all the above come and go. Often, they are remedied not long after individuals point them out—by the time this book is published, the errors described will likely be fixed, or the results changed somehow; such is the nature of constant updating and feedback. But the temporary nature of these factual errors and sociocultural biases is not the point; the point is that people trust these facts, which are on constantly shifting and unstable ground, without understanding the nature of these media. I list these examples and not many more in the book because they are numerous, and readers probably already understand the problem. This book explains where the information often comes from and the underlying media technologies that support it, along with some history and critical political economy—these, I think, are more helpful rather than simply listing errors.

Semantic Media

Historically, large media companies tend to monopolize markets to concentrate power and ownership (Bagdikian, 1983/2004). The same is true of contemporary internet companies that mediate information or are directly involved in media production (Mosco, 1996/2009; McChesney, 2013). Research has shown how capitalism shapes and influences products like search engines by privatizing search (Mager, 2012). Others describe a new era of semantic capitalism (Feuz et al., 2011; Floridi, 2018) where market logic bounds the mass production and transmission of meaning and facts. Scholars have analyzed the politics of these semantic infrastructures (Waller, 2016; Allhutter, 2019) as human-made technologies for knowledge automation and articulated the necessity of undertaking further political-economic analyses of their power and positioning in everyday social life.

Internet media companies attempt to present facts and "knowledge" to you because they want you to stay on their media product, interacting with their associated products, rather than leave to visit another business's products on the web. While companies like Google have historically sought to be the de facto information gateway leading people to other sources, such companies now directly provide users with answers to their questions. There are multiple ways that companies achieve this, and usually they connect to media technologies that specialize in maintaining semantics on the internet. Text-based search engines like those from Baidu, Google, Microsoft, Yahoo, and Yandex, as well as virtual assistants and voice search from Apple (Siri), Amazon (Alexa), Microsoft (Cortana), and Google (Google Assistant), all rely on technologies that retrieve and present facts for people. This retrieval of facts happens in various ways, sometimes from external and public websites, often from internal and proprietary databases of facts owned by these companies.

To be clear, the following bears repeating. Semantic media are less about searching for keywords and matches on different websites that are then ranked for you to choose. Instead, such media deal with identifying and describing entities (things like people, products, and places) and actions for interacting with those entities (things like purchasing, scheduling, and contacting). They leverage technologies not well known to the average internet user. Non-specialists don't understand how Google or Microsoft identify concepts and connect related information about them. How do companies produce facts and organize the data? From where does the data originate? What do these processes mean for web users and administrators? What types of gatekeeping or safety checks do companies perform?

Although this book's title explicitly mentions *semantic media*, it will also focus partly on semantic theory and technology to help understand how semantic media are informed and operate. Figure 0.3 describes these areas and the kinds of items each area covers. *Semantic theory* is lexical and conceptual, based on how specific rules and logic apply to words, theories of meaning, ontology (the philosophical study of being or what exists), and taxonomy. *Semantic technology* deals with metadata (data that indicate what other data are about), markup languages through which people write metadata (code), knowledge bases and graphs (databases), web schemas and applied ontologies (controlled vocabularies), and enterprise software (used by businesses and companies). "Ontology" is used in information science to denote a concrete way of organizing information; in this context, think of ontologies as a standardized set of metadata. These all contribute to

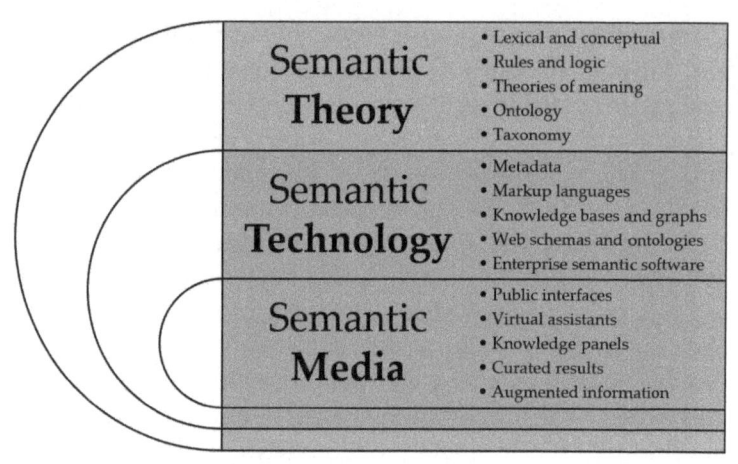

Figure 0.3: Overlapping foundations of semantic media

Source: Created by the author

and inform semantic media; the public interfaces (screens and dashboards), virtual assistants, knowledge panels, curated results, and, eventually, augmented information in emerging media products (Iliadis & Pedersen, 2018; Liao & Iliadis, 2021) that people interact with daily. Chapter 1 concentrates primarily on semantic theory, chapters 3 and 4 focus on semantic technology, and chapters 2 and 5 focus on semantic media products.

I am also interested in writing about companies' *data infrastructures* to see how they add facts to their products. Doing so will, I hope, increase what Gray et al. (2018) refer to as "data infrastructure literacy," that is, "the ability to account for, intervene around and participate in the wider socio-technical infrastructures through which data is created, stored and analysed." What do data infrastructures allow for, enable, and afford in the creation and transmission of facts in semantic media products? My interest is not only in things like Wikipedia but also Wikidata and DBpedia (databases of facts). I'm not only interested in Google but also Schema.org (a metadata vocabulary through which web administrators may tag and label facts) and Google's Knowledge Graph (their proprietary database). I'm interested not just in Facebook but also in Facebook's Open Graph (a method for organizing and labeling external web data within Facebook); not only Apple but Apple's Active Ontology (how Apple manages knowledge in products like Siri); and Microsoft and their Satori product and Concept Graph (how Microsoft taxonomizes knowledge). The list goes on, as we shall see.

Critique

I adopt a critical stance towards these contemporary media technologies, processes, and products and hope to raise issues about how organizations represent facts. These companies increasingly act as all-encompassing semantic information layers that present data from their internal databases and public websites in the form of facts. In this respect, they can push out smaller organizations that offer these services and depend on visitors interacting directly with their products. They also can distort and drown out local knowledge.

There is evidence to justify this critical attitude. As shown in an investigative report by *The Markup*, "41% of the first page of Google search results is taken up by Google products" (Jeffries & Yin, 2020). These practices led the US Department of Justice to file a federal lawsuit, accusing Google of "illegally monopolizing the market for search through anticompetitive behavior" (Jeffries, 2020). The filing states that "Google has taken steps to close the ecosystem from competition and insert itself as the middleman between app developers and consumers." Among Google's properties in its top search results, *The Markup* found that some included knowledge panels that "show summaries and facts drawn from the 'knowledge graph,' Google's database of facts and entities curated from various sources." According to a study cited in the reporting, customers often confuse where the content that populates these items comes from, confusing Google and Wikipedia information (McMahon et al., 2017). These types of knowledge panels and graphs are at Google, Facebook, and Amazon. As we shall see, a lot of infrastructure goes into these knowledge panels. The panels use things like proprietary databases (databases of facts the companies own), web schemas (which administrators use to mark up their pages for retrieval by these companies), and open data repositories (free to use data collections of publicly sourced facts). Companies use these to present facts in media products like the knowledge panels and virtual assistants described in this book.

Outline of the Book

The first chapter describes "a history" of semantic media (it is by no means meant to be exhaustive). It contains some information about the history of semantics, how semantics became embedded in computing technologies, and how they appeared on the web and internet media products. This history chapter describes critical events leading up to the semantic media in the rest of the book. It discusses some early history of the web, important people like Tim-Berners Lee, the role of metadata, the World Wide Web Consortium, the Semantic Web movement, linked data, and the subjects, predicates, and objects that make up semantic media. The chapter focuses on the early aspirations that semantic engineers had for their technologies and infrastructures.

The second chapter discusses the transition from an open semantic web to a web semantics of walled gardens and gatekeepers. It outlines how large internet companies use proprietary knowledge graphs to endow their media products with semantics. It focuses on Google's Knowledge Graph (among other knowledge graphs) and knowledge base technologies and how they shape media use and adoption processes. If the first generation of search involved retrieving information and providing ordered lists of links to that information, the next generation of search involved extracting facts and serving them to users who no longer click through to primary sources. The chapter also discusses knowledge graphs at IBM and those created by Airbnb, Uber, Microsoft, and Amazon.

The third chapter dives into a specific case study and methodology and discusses the Schema.org project, the first genuinely universal semantic metadata vocabulary for the web. I describe how Schema.org appears to be open and public but is more like a Google-run property. This chapter is about data infrastructures on the internet and how Schema.org represents a change on the web. We will discuss what Schema.org means socially and politically for web developers and users. Schema.org extends and assists things like the knowledge graphs described in the second chapter and virtual assistants described in the fifth chapter.

The fourth chapter discusses a second case study by examining Wikidata (an open-source knowledge base tied to Wikipedia) and its use as a data source for semantic media like virtual assistants and knowledge panels. It examines Wikidata's structure and the nature of the "facts" that it contains, which attempt to codify the knowledge inside of Wikipedia using semantic technologies. We'll look at the project's history, how the technology operates, and what it means for internet users. We'll also look at some sociocultural biases and ethical issues connected to the project. Wikidata is a different type of technology than the one described in the third chapter. Schema.org is a metadata vocabulary that can mark up pages on the web to retrieve facts from them. Wikidata is a knowledge base of facts that people can also query for results.

The fifth and final chapter looks at the virtual assistants that benefit from the technologies described in the rest of the book. It provides some historical context for under-standing the development of virtual assistants like Siri and Alexa. It explains how they internally organize categories and source information from places like knowledge graphs,

Schema.org, and Wikidata to help answer questions for people. These tools rely on the types of products discussed in the previous three chapters. We'll learn a little about the history of these technologies and how they are a form of semantic media.

The material in this book is based on years of research, interviews, attending and presenting at academic and industry conferences, researching semantic theory, technology, and media, and conversations with scholars focusing on machines that communicate meaningfully. The conclusion is that media platforms are not only the products of algorithms—things like statistical processes and machine learning—but are also the product of logical data modeling decisions that inform these media. "Algorithms" has become a misnomer, encapsulating various disparate media technologies. Artificial intelligence is not only about machine learning, natural language processing, robotics, and visualization; it is also about logic, symbols, and knowledge representation. Data modeling is a crucial feature of emerging media that becomes hidden behind contemporary debates about algorithms, which are only half of an explanation for how modern media systems on the internet operate. Future research should be attentive to this more often obscured side of contemporary media technologies, which offer innumerable opportunities to study and amend their shortcomings.

1

A History of Semantics

In Virginia Woolf's 1931 experimental novel *The Waves*, the character Neville says: "Nothing should be named lest by so doing we change it." This line has resonated with me ever since I read it as a college student. From sunrise to sunset, Neville and the other characters lounge around somewhere in England, discussing weighty philosophical topics like life, love, death, identity, and language in a dreamlike and breezy coastal scene. The book's treatment of the last of these topics—language—interested me most. Neville continues: "Let it exist, this bank, this beauty, and I, for one instant, steeped in pleasure. The sun is hot. I see the river. I see trees specked and burnt in the autumn sunlight." Neville seems to be saying something profound about the nature of language—that language can be both representative and restrictive. He says that life could not be commensurate with or contained in language. Later in the same passage, Neville hints that language can be too much: "Words and words and words, how they gallop." Truth, *The Waves* seems to be saying, necessarily exceeds language's attempt to represent or capture it.

Early Semantics

Beyond modernist fiction and outside of the traditions of rhetoric and speculative etymology, the study of language as a philosophical area of inquiry in the modern era begins roughly in the late seventeenth century with the work of the French linguist Michel Bréal (1832–1915), particularly in his 1897 book *Essai de sémantique*. The word *semantics* primarily comes to us from Bréal's book, a comprehensive study of the psychology of language. *Sémantique* itself comes from the Greek words *semantikos*, meaning "significant," *semainein*, meaning "to show by sign, signify, point out, indicate by a sign," and *sema*, meaning "sign, mark, or token." While language study was already underway in the late-1800s, Bréal writes that most studies focused on syntax (things like linking vowels or the order of terms) rather than on semantics and the *meaning* of words, which Bréal regarded as most important. For Bréal, the field of Semantics (with a capital "S") was to be concerned with "the science of meaning." Geeraerts (2009) outlines some distinctive features of Bréal's philological semantic project, noting that semantics began with Bréal as a historical and interpretive discipline that highlighted a psychological orientation to the study of meaning.

Meaning obviously can be found and discussed in ways beyond words, including formal and mathematical logic, actions, visual imagery, and music. When people discuss computational semantics today, it usually concerns lexical semantics relating to words or vocabulary—several disciplines study varieties of lexical semantics, including philosophy, linguistics, and computer science. My particular interest is in how large internet companies are now leveraging lexical-semantic technologies to build and release popular products that we use every day. The rest of this chapter will take you on a brief journey through significant historical moments in theoretical semantics before transitioning to a history of how semantics became embedded in web and internet technologies.

Apart from Bréal, two other historical figures had a significant early influence on semantics, or what they would have called the discipline of *semiotics*, or the formal study of signs and sign systems. The first was a student of Bréal, the Swiss linguist Ferdinand de Saussure (1857–1913), also informally known as the "father" of modern linguistics. The ideas of de Saussure introduced *structuralism* to semantics (moving beyond the historical and interpretive methods of his teacher, Bréal). In de Saussure's version of semiotics, language connects to the human activity of creating social symbols and facts. It is a "system of signs that express ideas," not unlike writing systems. He advocated for science that studies the social life of linguistic signs called *semiology*. In his best-known work, *Cours de linguistique générale* [*Course in general linguistics*], these ideas were published posthumously in 1916 by his former students (based on notes from his lectures at the University of Geneva from 1906 to 1911). The structuralist semantics de Saussure proposed emphasized the analysis of meaning through a tripartite relationship consisting of *sign*, *signified*, and *signifier*. For example, if someone gives a rose on Valentine's Day, the signifier would be the *rose*, the signified would be *love*, and both together would produce the sign *I love you* that someone gives on Valentine's Day. An intriguing aspect of de Saussure's semiology is that these signs are entirely arbitrary; a sign can be made up of any signifier and signified since these depend on socially constructed meanings.

The second well-known historical figure to influence semantics through something like a triadic system was the American philosopher Charles Sanders Peirce (1839–1914). Peirce developed a similar theory of signs called *semeiotic* concurrently, if not slightly ahead of Bréal and de Saussure. As Houser (1992) explains, in Peirce's version, a sign is something that stands *for* something (an object) *to* something else (an interpretant). The three elements are different between the two thinkers, but the relational and social dimensions remain the same. Some of Peirce's earliest reflections on this process, or what he calls *semeiosis*, are presented in "What is a sign?" (1894/1998) and "Of reasoning in general" (1895/1998). There, he discusses how signs can consist of things like *icons*, *indices*, or *symbols*. An icon would be an image, and an index would be a scale such as a measurement. A symbol would be something like the word "loves" used in a sentence to describe a relationship between two people. While similar, de Saussure's work would primarily influence structuralist linguistics in the twentieth century. In contrast, Peirce's influence arguably belongs to the field of philosophy.[9]

The works of Bréal, de Saussure, and Peirce represent just three (and thus limited) essential research programs in the history of semantics; semantics research went through multiple transformational developments over the twentieth century. Today, semantics is a fully developed subject with several subfields and is taught in textbooks focusing on subareas such as *conceptual* and *cognitive* semantics, to name only two (Riemer, 2010). This chapter will now focus on a few critical terms from the history of philosophy, which help explain how lexical semantics applies to computers. We'll then go on to cover a variety of ways these terms apply to semantic technologies on the internet.

Ontological Semantics

Lexical semantics, as we have so far described it (word meanings and word relations), is intimately tied to ontology and logic. As mentioned earlier, ontology is the branch of philosophy that studies what kinds of entities exist in the world and describes their relationships. Logic is a type of thinking that assumes that people can create facts and statements about those entities and relations by identifying objects (things or nouns) and predicates (actions or verbs), which can also be variables. Let's say that semantics is about word meanings and word relations in specific contexts. There must be occasions where there is at least some baseline ontological agreement about what *kinds of things* there are and how we name these entities and articulate their *relationships* through lexical processes of word description.

Ontology typically deals with identifying entities, properties, relations, and states of affairs and events, and philosophers will usually describe these things using different kinds of logic. These include discussions of *universals* vs. *particulars* (types vs. instances, e.g., a headache vs. Erica's headache); *taxonomies* (classification hierarchies such as those handed down by Aristotle and Linnaeus: think of how biology defines species); *mereology* (identifying parthood relations like part_of, has_part, overlaps_with, etc.); *topology* (spatial relations like boundary_of, connected_to, adjacent_to, etc.); and *dependence* (essence relations such as inheres_in, bearer_of, etc.). Philosophical ontology thus provides analytical tools for the demarking of specific entities and associations expressed in logic, which helps us understand factual statements. For example, to semantically analyze the meaning of the phrase "Amelia is a member of the local library," I need to identify the subjects and predicates in the sentence, who and what they are, and their relationship. Philosophical ontology helps break down these components, especially when there are many entities and the connections are complex (such as in the field of bioinformatics, for example).

While philosophers have studied ontology since antiquity, the twentieth century saw an increase in ontology works, particularly ontology's links to language and semantics (meaning). The American philosopher Willard Van Orman Quine famously highlighted the notion of *ontological commitment* in a paper from 1948 titled "On what there is," where he described how, to be accurate, an ontological theory about things that exist need only be "true" concerning the relations between objects and predicates that are related and *committed to in the theory*. Here, truth is a condition that depends on the semantic structure of the ontological theory. An ontological commitment to *object X* must also involve the *predicate of X*. Different ontologies can define and describe different sets of objects and relations, and sometimes these may seem incompatible. This situation is because, as Quine saw it, any ontological theory must first commit to particular kinds of objects and relations. It would not make sense to compare ontologies because "truth" lies in an ontological theory's internal commitments rather than in another theory. Language thus plays a crucial role in thinking about ontology. In referring to ontology, Quine describes it as "operating on a semantical plane."

Around the same time, in 1950, the German philosopher of language Rudolf Carnap (Carnap was a member of the Vienna Circle) released a paper titled "Empiricism, semantics, and ontology." Carnap wrote that "semantics in the technical sense is still in the initial phases of its development, and we must be prepared for possible fundamental changes in methods." In 1952, Carnap and Yehoshua Bar-Hillel (Bar-Hillel was an Israeli philosopher and mathematician who focused on linguistics and machine translation) published "An outline of a theory of semantic information." They contrast this publication with a much more famous communication theory, Claude Shannon's 1948 landmark "A mathematical theory of communication." Shannon's theory largely ignores semantics and meaning problems by treating communication as an informational measure of the *statistical probability* of a signal. Realizing that Shannon's theory did not account for semantics, Carnap and Bar-Hillel wrote that "semantic information is a concept more readily applicable to psychological and other investigations than its communicational counterpart." Like others at the time, they identified the importance of semantic information in communication processes. Shannon himself had already acknowledged that his mathematical theory of communication did not and could not account for all the various ways that one could use the concept of information to communicate, including via semantics (meaning). Floridi (2011) explains these information modalities, including the distinctions articulated by Shannon, Carnap, and Bar-Hillel.[10]

Subjects, Predicates, Objects

As mentioned in the introduction, the emphasis in this book is on the *media* part of the term semantic media (media technologies, specifically), so I'll limit myself to describing only the most foundational aspects of theoretical semantics discussed in the rest of the book. The terms *subject*, *predicate*, and *object* are central to lexical semantics and are particularly important for understanding how semantics exists in semantic media products. Subjects are typically *noun* entities and describe the "who" or "what" of a statement, and predicates are usually *verbs* and explain things like "actions." Objects are also often noun entities to which the action of subjects refers. These terms are collectively called "semantic triples" or simply "triples." They are the building blocks of lexical semantics and logic that can isolate, break down, and analyze factual statements. Using the example referred to above, when I say "Amelia is a member of the local library," then, in this statement, "Amelia" is the *subject*, "is_a member" is the *predicate*, and "local library" is the object. These statements can be codified in machine languages to help create "meaning" that machines can "recognize" and share with users. Figure 1.1 shows the three main components of these semantic triples.

One can relate these semantics using lower or higher degrees of complexity and expressivity. For example, Obrst (2003) describes how ontologies for semantics

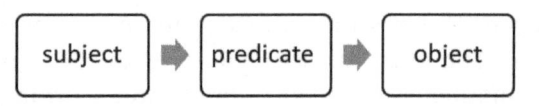

Figure 1.1: Semantic triple

Source: Created by the author

can be expressed weakly through things like *taxonomy* and *thesauri* (think of things like book indexes or library catalogs that identify "parent" and "child" relationships). Or they can be expressed more strongly through *logical theories* (think of the complex varieties of ontological logic discussed in the previous section). Semantic syntax languages codify these stronger logics so machines can "understand" logical definitions and relationships of data related to things in the world. For example, we all know that the following hypothetical scenario occurs daily. Some of our friends are on social media. These friends have demographic information uploaded there, and they regularly do things like share links and interact with their friends' posts (by liking them, etc.). This information is expressed, stored, and queried using codified semantic languages by anyone who has access to the data. It is possible, for example, for Facebook or Instagram to run queries looking for ontologically complex semantic statements. Examples might be "24-year-old females in Chicago who like vegan food and punk music," or for Google to run a search for something like "The best Greek restaurants near The Beaches neighborhood in Toronto that serve spanokopita."

The media technologies that we use every day depend on lexical-semantic parsing. For example, *structured data modeling* (data organization practices for storing and managing information) and *natural language processing* (automatically processing our voices and words) coexist in internet products. Both will typically involve at least some form of identifying subjects, predicates, and objects. On the structured data side, metadata (data that describe other data), web schemas (shared vocabularies for tagging web data), knowledge graphs (organized information captured from multiple sources in graph form), and applied ontologies (a regulated set of metadata) all include semantics to improve machine "understanding." For example, a web developer may use a manually created metadata schema so that search engines find information on the site more efficiently to display in menus like knowledge panels. On the natural language side, speech recognition (the automatic identification and translation of vocal utterances), part of speech tagging (grammatical labeling of words based on definition and context), and word sense disambiguation (isolating which specific senses of terms are in sentences) exist. Also performed here are named entity recognition (classifying recognizable people, places, and things in language), co-reference resolution (finding all instances where expressions refer to the same entity), sentiment analysis (indicating affective states based on words), and natural language generation (the automatic production of language by an artificial agent). All include semantic processes to "understand" what people are saying (e.g., a virtual assistant will engage in named entity recognition to identify essential terms uttered and assign them to slots like "movie" or "restaurant").

A critical distinction between the two approaches discussed above is that one group primarily uses *statistics* (probabilities) to parse semantics in unstructured data on the web (natural language processing). In contrast, the other uses *logic* (reason) to create structured data that machines can parse to get at the underlying semantics (structured data modeling). Both approaches often work together in the semantic media products we use. I will skew towards examining the logic and structured data side because I am primarily interested in how media products holistically communicate semantic facts and meaning. I am less interested in the automated generation of textual highlights and keywords in the language of search results (though we will also briefly discuss some underlying natural language processing techniques). Thus, I focus on semantic media that use structured data for the networked expression of facts and meaning rather than machine learning.[11]

Computational Semantics

I mentioned earlier that philosophers and logicians assume that some facts and statements made by people are in the form of semantic triples—but this is only half the story in the history of semantics. The other, perhaps more important, is that logicians and programmers tried to devise computational systems through which symbols can express objects, predicates, and variables. People could then manipulate these symbols based on their forms and according to rules that would produce an "accurate" reasoning pattern. In this version of computational semantics, the formal nature of the logic was essential, not only because it lead to automated reasoning but because it provided a way to investigate the "accuracy" of reasoning, avoid miscommunication, and decrease ambiguity. Philosophers such as Carnap and fellow Vienna Circle member Otto Neurath (Neurath was also the Editor-in-Chief of the *Encyclopedia of Unified Science*) thought such practices would lead to research collaborations to solve global problems. That vision informs the work of computational semantics investigators today.

Semantics has been a part of computing since the 1950s and the development of *distributional semantics* and *semantic networks*. Around that time, the Austrian philosopher Ludwig Wittgenstein released his *Philosophical Investigations* (1953). Wittgenstein described understanding the world as limited to "language-games" (*Sprachspiel*) where words only have meaning in their usage contexts and according to language rules and our understandings of those rules. Distributional semantics is a similar linguistic idea handed down by the British linguist John Rupert Firth, who said that "a word is characterized by the company it keeps" (1957). Firth meant that words make sense in terms of the other words connected to in contexts like sentences (the idea is that you can learn a lot about words in their relation to each other). The term "fish" on its own may carry some information, whereas it has more if we examine the word in sentences like "She caught a big fish in the Mediterranean Sea that day" or "He was fishing for compliments." Certain words are identified and weighted next to "fish" in these sentences that tell us more about the entity "fish" in each of the two specific contexts, where "fish" expresses something slightly different.

Such focus on words and their meaning as they exist in a distributional space is related to a critical concept in computing called semantic networks. Semantic networks are a knowledge representation technology that uses nodes (which represent entities) and links (which define relationships between entities) to visualize knowledge of entities and their relationships. These networks help us to imagine "knowledge" graphically. Nodes, or *vertices* (points), can be things like noun entity subjects and objects discussed above, and links, or *edges* (lines), can be verbs or actions like predicates. Semantic networks can be produced in visualizations such as conceptual mapping or graph databases and are helpful in various processes, including structured data modeling and natural language processing. An in-depth example of a semantic network is presented in chapter 3, where we'll discuss the Schema.org project as a case study.

Like semantic networks, early work in artificial intelligence focused on the problem of how to represent knowledge in computers through logic graphically. Researchers wondered if machines could then act on the understanding programmed on them. For example, in the United States, the computer scientist John McCarthy (McCarthy is known as one of the founders of AI) described programming knowledge representations into machines using logic in a piece from 1958 titled "Programs with common sense." He wrote that an imagined advice taker (a computer) would be a "program for solving problems by manipulating sentences in formal languages" and that "its behavior will be improvable merely by making statements to it, telling it about its symbolic environment." The machine would be taught "facts" in logical statements such as the triples described earlier in this chapter. McCarthy uses the examples of teaching a computer that a *home is walkable* ("walkable(home)") and that a *county is drivable* ("drivable(county)"). The computer could then use these abstract logical representations to make decisions when answering questions.

McCarthy founded the Stanford Artificial Intelligence Laboratory (SAIL) in 1963, later joined by Ed Feigenbaum. Feigenbaum was another early AI researcher and computer scientist who many people credit with founding the field of *expert systems*. In such scenarios, computers help make complex decisions based on data that computer scientists program into them. Feigenbaum created the Knowledge Systems Laboratory (KSL) within SAIL, dedicated to advancing research in technological knowledge representation. Many researchers credit Feigenbaum and the programs he established at KSL with turning the focus of AI research away from reasoning algorithms and toward knowledge representation in knowledge bases.

Programming machines with something like common sense through concepts and logical reasoning proved to be an enduring theme throughout the 1970s and 1980s. The American researcher William Woods released "What's in a link: Foundations for semantic networks" in 1975. There, he discusses "the theoretical underpinnings for semantic network representations." He describes the "intended meanings for various types of arcs and links, the need for careful thought in [...] representing facts as assemblages of arcs and nodes, and [...] problems in knowledge representation" (Woods would later go on to work as a software engineer at Google).

In 1976, the American computer scientist John Sowa published his influential "Conceptual graphs for a data base interface," which describes how to represent general concepts in a machine that would eliminate the need for certain users to learn coding languages. He wrote that *conceptual graphs* "could support an interface that would let the user talk about familiar data in a familiar terminology without the need for special query languages." Sowa elaborates on these ideas in *Conceptual structures: Information processing in mind and machine* (1984). Around the same time, Doug Lenat, another early AI researcher, popularized logic and common sense in machines. Lenat began work on expert systems and knowledge-based systems described in the books (with Randall Davis) *Knowledge-based systems in artificial intelligence* (1982) and (with Frederick Hayes-Roth and Donald Waterman) *Building expert systems* (1983). Lenat would describe the practice of teaching machines common sense through logical reasoning as "ontological engineering" (1989)—see the *Wired* article about Lenat, "One genius' lonely crusade to teach a computer common sense" (Metz, 2016). Early expert systems included products like Mycin, a rule-based approach to providing an expert diagnosis of bacterial infections, and recommended courses of treatment (Ribes et al., 2019; Chari et al., 2020a).

Another early contributor was one of McCarthy and Feigenbaum's students at Stanford, Ramanathan Guha. Guha worked on projects with Lenat, including Cyc (Lenat et al., 1985, 1990; Lenat, 1995), an artificial intelligence project that uses various types of expressive logic to encode something like common sense understanding into machines. For example, "if you hold a cup of coffee upside down, the coffee will fall out." This semantic reasoning is different from machine learning, which produces automated language translation or language searching tasks, where the goal is to find connections through statistical learning and probability. Here, the focus is on logical rules of thumb that tell a computer how the world works using human common sense, thus producing something like a computational version of "knowledge" where computers can make inferences about the world. In 1989, Lenat and Guha published *Building large knowledge-based systems: Representation and inference in the Cyc project*. Guha would eventually land a job at Google to develop Google Custom Search and currently works as a Google Fellow. In 1993, Guha and co-authors Rob McCool and Eric Miller presented a paper titled "Semantic search," which describes building on semantic technologies to improve traditional web searching with knowledge representations (Guha et al., 2003).

Finally, we should end this early computer history with WordNet. WordNet began in the early 1990s at the Cognitive Science Laboratory of Princeton University under the supervision of George Miller and Christiane Fellbaum. WordNet is a lexical database of semantic relations between words. Today, it contains more than 200 languages (Miller et al., 1990; Miller, 1995) and is helpful for several computing tasks since it includes a sizeable semantic dataset. WordNet will tell a user the semantic relations between words in terms of *hyponymy*, meaning hyponyms (subtypes), and hypernyms (supertypes). For example, "baby's breath" is a subtype of the supertype "flower." WordNet has remained an essential resource for semantic projects requiring a large training set of words and their relationships to conduct different processing tasks.

The Semantic Web

Perhaps the most important and controversial aspect of computational semantics concerning the content in this book is what is known as the *semantic web*. Before we dive into some of the semantic web's history, let us simply say that the semantic web helped popularize the idea of, and develop the technologies for, representing things like semantic triples on the web. Figure 1.2 shows

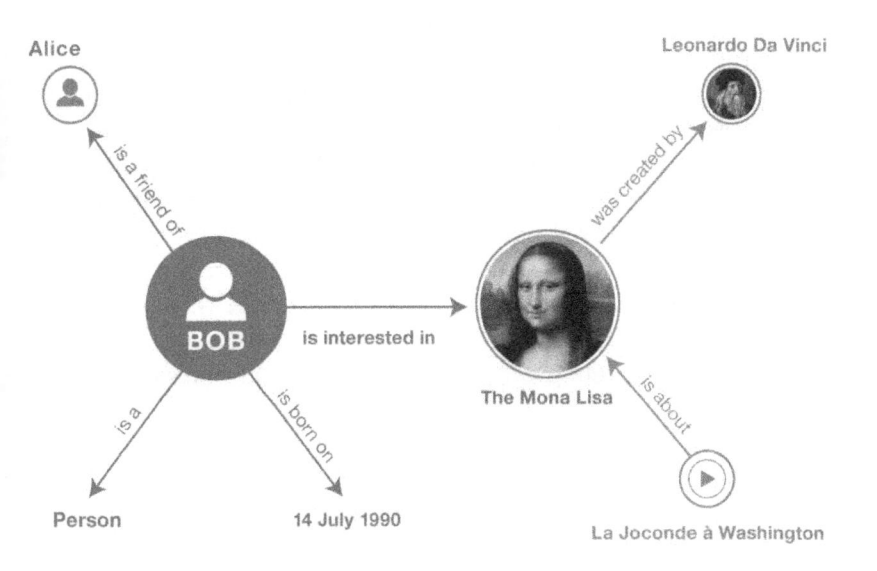

```
<Bob> <is a> <person>.
<Bob> <is a friend of> <Alice>.
<Bob> <is born on> <the 4th of July 1990>.
<Bob> <is interested in> <the Mona Lisa>.
<Leonardo da Vinci> <is the creator of> <the Mona Lisa>.
<The video 'La Joconde à Washington'> <is about> <the Mona Lisa>
```

```
01    {
02       "@context": "example-context.json",
03       "@id": "http://example.org/bob#me",
04       "@type": "Person",
05       "birthdate": "1990-07-04",
06       "knows": "http://example.org/alice#me",
07       "interest": {
08          "@id": "http://www.wikidata.org/entity/Q12418",
09          "title": "Mona Lisa",
10          "subject_of":
"http://data.europeana.eu/item/04802/243FA8618938F4117025F17A8B813C
5F9AA4D619",
11          "creator":
"http://dbpedia.org/resource/Leonardo_da_Vinci"
12       }
13    }
```

Figure 1.2: From top: semantic triples as network, list, and code

three representations of "knowledge" codified in semantic triples.

In the example, semantic triples represent the following facts: a person named Bob has a birth date of July 14, 1990, is a friend of someone named Alice, has an interest in the painting *Mona Lisa*, which Leonardo Da Vinci created, and this painting is the subject of a video called *La Joconde à Washington*. These facts are displayable as a network (top), as a list (middle), and through code (bottom). The semantic web project focuses on this kind of data modeling on the web to help computers "understand" certain types of facts.

The semantic web began as an interconnected group of technologies, standards, and methods for improving data interoperability across the web (Calaresu & Shiri, 2015). In 1999, web inventor Sir Tim Berners-Lee expressed that "the first form of semantic data on the Web was metadata" (Berners-Lee and Fischetti, 1999). After inventing the web in 1989, Berners-Lee founded the World Wide Web Consortium (W3C) in 1994, a leading international standards organization for the web. W3C describes the semantic web as a *web of data* (Hogan, 2020). The group has led several semantic web initiatives, publishing standards such as the Resource Description Framework (RDF) data model (Lassila & Swick, 1999) like the kind displayed in figure 1.2 (Schreiber & Raimond, 2014). The model identifies (as mentioned previously) subjects (i.e., the "who" or "what"), predicates (i.e., "verbs" or "actions"), and objects (i.e., noun "entities" to which subjects direct the actions). W3C also develops the coding languages through which the RDF model is serialized to describe semantics, including iterations of the widely used Web Ontology Language (OWL) and the more recent Shapes Constraint Language (SHACL) (see w3.org). OWL is a knowledge representation language that can write ontologies (McGuinness & van Harmelen, 2004), and SHACL is "a language for validating RDF graphs against a set of conditions" (Knublauch & Kontokostas,

2017). The SPARQL Protocol and RDF Query Language (SPARQL—a recursive acronym), also released via W3C, is used to look up RDF searches and run queries on the graph (Prud'hommeaux & Seaborne, 2008).

An early precursor to RDF was the Meta Content Framework (MCF). MCF was a format for representing web information through metadata modeling. Guha developed it at Apple in the mid-1990s; Guha, recall, had worked with Lenat on early symbolic artificial intelligence research with the Cyc project. Before developing MCF, he had recently finished his 1992 dissertation at Stanford on representing contexts in knowledge representation applications (Guha, 1992). Guha later left Apple for Netscape (before the move to Google) and worked with Tim Bray to instantiate MCF in W3C's Extensible Markup Language (XML) (Guha & Bray, 1997; Bray et al., 1997), a markup language for encoding web documents (Bray et al., 1997). Bray also worked for Google and eventually ended up at Amazon before leaving the company in 2020. Other work in semantic web markup languages came out of military research funding of projects such as the Defense Advanced Research Projects Agency's (DARPA) Agent Markup Language (DAML), which was started in 1999 by a team of researchers led by Jim Hendler. DAML and another project, the Ontology Inference Layer (OIL), created by Dieter Fensel, Frank van Harmelen, and Ian Horrocks (Fensel et al., 2001), would eventually fuse to become OWL (Hendler & McGuinness, 2000).

In 2001, Berners-Lee, Hendler, and Ora Lassila (Lassila helped lead the RDF project with Ralph Swick and eventually became Principal Graph Technologist at Amazon Web Services) published what would become the most widely read and cited article about the semantic web. The cover article is titled "The semantic web" in an issue of *Scientific American* (Berners-Lee et al., 2001). It is perhaps with this single article in mind that many casual observers of internet history have formed opinions about the semantic web—including that it is a "failed" or "dead" project (Target, 2018). As we shall see, the "semantic web" as a linguistic term was a type of branding exercise. Later ways to describe the same group of technologies went by names like "linked data" and "knowledge graphs" (the term that has become popular after large internet companies like Google started using it). We'll talk more about the knowledge graphs of internet companies in the next chapter.

In 2006, Berners-Lee famously issued four rules for an *open* and *public* semantic web that could verify against a five-star *linked data* system. The original dream of the semantic web was that it would help link data transparently across the internet for the benefit of all society. These rules included using Uniform Resource Identifiers (URIs) as names for items (basically something like a serial number) and using Hypertext Transfer Protocol (HTTP) URIs so individuals can look up words. Metadata was to engage the RDF model and include links to enable discovery by web users. According to Berners-Lee, a five-star linked open data rating from W3C would require that the data be open licensed and available as machine-readable structured data. It should also exist in a non-proprietary format, use W3C technical standards for identifying data, and link the data, thus creating a context (Berners-Lee, 2006). Since then, W3C's standards have bootstrapped the semantic web, undergirding web data in several industries.

A patent for the semantic web, titled "System and method for creating a semantic web and its applications in browsing, searching, profiling, personalization and advertising" (Sheth et al., 2001), was filed only a few short years after Google's founding. While Google is still around, there is an agreement in some corners that the semantic web is no longer "relevant." Some have this opinion partly because of how the semantic web was initially dreamt of and framed. It was marketed as an ideal way for everyday web developers and even more casual users to semantically mark up their web information. Tools and standards came and went in the intervening years, some fluctuating in popularity, thus failing to achieve critical mass with the public the way that the original minds behind the semantic web imagined they would. Another reason could arguably be a lack of return on investment; web developers could use semantic technologies to mark up information, but where were the popular everyday products that would take advantage of them? There were no media products like virtual assistants and knowledge panels to use these semantic facts and relay them to users.

There is, perhaps, a third reason the semantic web idea never took off the way that some people anticipated. Semantic web technologies can seem confusing to the more casual web developer. Not every user had a background in logic, nor did they have the time to learn and understand the many standards, syntaxes, and protocols. Berners-Lee originally envisioned the semantic web and transparent web data exchange as an open and democratic public resource. While the semantic web project has yet to achieve the vision of ubiquitous public adoption, there is clear evidence that specific standards and tools created by W3C have become leveraged or imitated in the enterprise, proprietary technologies, and privatized industries. Thus, the semantic web's initial public mandate expressed by its founders is partially inverted (Hitzler, 2021). Yet, governments, financial and news industries, and health researchers have widely used the technologies, too. However, historical narratives of the project's failure often exclude these domains and their successful use of semantic web technologies.

The semantic web as a concept and set of technologies has a messy internet history. As McCarthy (2017) shows, a series of "entangled" semantic webs might more accurately describe the semantic web project, due in part to the diverse, specialized industries where idiosyncratic vocabularies are in use (commerce, publishing, etc.). There are also tensions between proprietary and public metadata schemas. This heterogeneity of semantic web resources is why the project can arguably be said to have failed in its original vision. However, as we shall see, the project is finding a new life owing to large media companies. The continued use of these tools has created a new set of social and political problems that need addressing beyond the technical resistance from casual web developers who find the technology cumbersome. Researchers have voiced concerns about the attempt to create universal semantics for the web through specific web vocabularies. Reagle (1999) discusses legal considerations of these designs from the perspective of language, and Golumbia (2009) discusses the shortcomings of the semantic web in its "majoritarian" quest to computerize English and translate other languages into English. Further historical and philosophical foundations of the semantic web, including some critiques, have been documented by researchers (Guns, 2013; Halpin, 2013; Halpin & Monnin 2014).

Yet, tools that came out of the semantic web project are in use today. The Linked Open Data Cloud project (figure 1.3a) shows many datasets on the internet marked up with semantic web code, thus making them interoperable and ready to be queried by numerous services (such as apps, virtual assistants, etc.). The diagram contains 1,301 datasets with 16,283 links, including datasets in domains such as geography, government, life sciences, linguistics, media, publications, and social networking (included among them are Wikidata and DBpedia, which we will discuss in chapter 4). While those numbers may not seem particularly large, these datasets are massive, and some have billions of facts represented in them. Some datasets contain crucial political information (such as the Ordnance Survey Linked Data Platform from Great Britain's national mapping agency, the Scottish Environment Protection Agency, and other open access resources to Scotland's official statistics, etc.). These data can be called and represented thanks to the semantic markup.

The Linked Open Vocabularies project (figure 1.3b) displays the more widely used ontology vocabularies

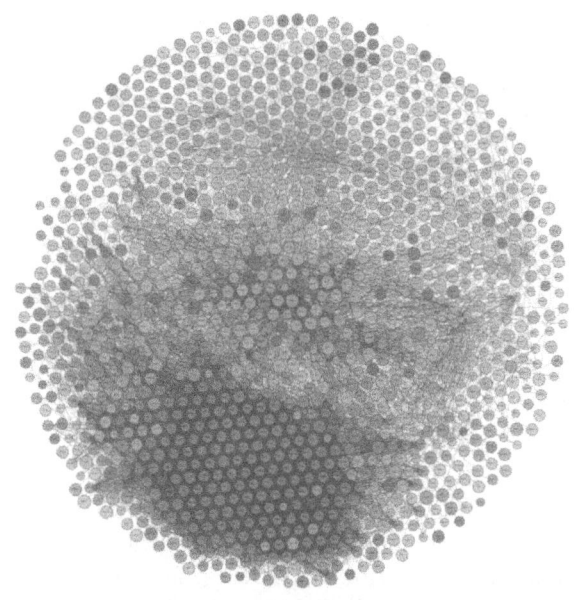

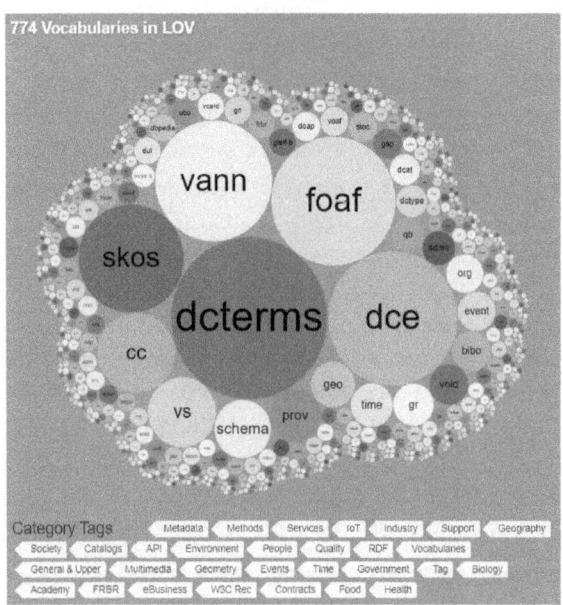

Figure 1.3: From top: Linked Open Data Cloud (lod-cloud.net), Linked Open Vocabularies (lov.linkeddata.es/dataset/lov).

(schemas) used to codify semantics into things like the datasets listed above in the Linked Open Data Cloud. These include individual pieces of information found on the web in websites, emails, applications, and platforms (Vandenbussche et al., 2017). There are currently 760 vocabularies, the largest of which is Dublin Core (terms used for describing *resources*). Friend of a Friend (terms used for expressing *society* like people, activities, and relationships) and more general languages such as the Simple Knowledge Organization System (SKOS) and Schema.org are also present. The latter is becoming the de facto schema, as it is in heavy use by internet search engines and virtual assistants (we will discuss Schema.org as a case study in chapter 3). Additionally, the Gartner industry report, which contains the infamous "hype cycle," has listed semantic technologies such as those described above in one form or another in several of its yearly reports. Such industry reports are speculative forecasting of technology used to hype the industry about emerging technologies.

A vital point of this book is that large internet companies also now use tools and ideas based on semantic web technologies. For example, Google released a paper in 2010 titled "How Google is using linked data today and vision for tomorrow" (Steiner et al., 2010). The article describes "how modern search engines, such as Google, make use of Linked Data spread in Web pages for displaying Rich Snippets" and how these might extend into future multimedia documents. "Rich snippets" is a term that Google uses to refer to the bits of information and details extracted from websites and surfaced directly in Google search results in panels and boxes. The paper states that several "semantic mark-up formats are supported by Google," including those based on RDF. It includes images and examples of these semantic markup languages populating rich structured details in Google search results.

In the following chapters, I will discuss three products that Google and other companies use based on this kind of semantic markup, including their proprietary knowledge graphs (chapter 2) and open-source produce like Schema. org (chapter 3) and Wikidata (chapter 4).

Language Models

While a lot of work is in semantic markup, companies like Google have also focused (some would say to a much greater degree) on pre-trained language models. Pre-trained language models are a vastly different approach from what I described above. These models use statistical modeling that trains a language model on a large set of data and then applies it to other instances or prompts of unstructured or natural language data to see how it will perform. For example, the model may be trained on all the books in Google Books and then use what it has learned to provide best-guess answers to people's questions based on probability functions. The machine learning algorithms in these models can automatically orchestrate unstructured data into meaningful facts by extracting things like subjects, predicates, and objects using different processes. These processes include those discussed earlier, such as word sense disambiguation (which sense of a word is in a sentence), part of speech tagging (labeling parts of sentences and terms according to their technical descriptions), and entity extraction, resolution, and linking (finding "things" in the text like people, places, times, organizations, etc.). The extracted data can then feed into a semantic knowledge base that stores facts in subjects, predicates, and objects (triples). Sometimes the facts in these databases are automatically parsed using these machine learning methods, and other times they are based on human-curated semantic data markup.

Research from projects like the previously mentioned WordNet would prove crucial for the latest technological advancements in natural language processing, such as *word embeddings*. Somewhat building on the ideas of distributional semantics and semantic networks developed half a century earlier, these focus on processing word representations in text analysis according to a statistical score that compares the meaning of words in terms of how close they are to each other. Based on the matched numbers assigned to each word, the assumption is that the words are more comparable in meaning if their numbers are closer in the space. In modern-day language models, these word vectors are trained over large datasets to produce statistical probabilities about word meanings, frequencies, and occurrences that can predict and generate words given only a little bit of input. The most relevant of these was Word2vec, created by a team of researchers led by Tomas Mikolov at Google in 2013, which is a technique for processing natural language that uses an algorithm to learn word meanings and associations and which would go on to influence technologies used by Google today (Mikolov et al., 2013).

Internet companies use language models like Google AI's Bidirectional Encoder Representations from Transformer (BERT) (Devlin et al., 2019) and Facebook AI's Bidirectional and Auto-Regressive Transformers (BART) (Lewis et al., 2020). Several other recently released models include the Generative Pre-trained Transformers from Open AI, GPT-2 (Radford et al., 2019) and GPT-3 (Brown et al., 2020). This work is expanding beyond language-only models currently. Google's recent Multitask Unified Model (MUM) update uses transformers trained in 75 languages and multimodal media such as images and expands to video (Raffel et al., 2019).

These models are trained on large datasets and are vulnerable to sociocultural biases and errors (Huang et al., 2019; Nadeem et al., 2020; Postigo, 2021). Such errors are why structured data modeling is arguably better for representing facts and organizing information. To that point, scientists at Google Research, DeepMind, and others have described combining these types of automated and statistical language model approaches with symbolic and logical approaches such as those presented in the semantic markup of knowledge bases described above to improve search (Battaglia et al., 2018; Erekhinskaya et al., 2020; Metzler et al., 2021; Yasunaga et al., 2021).

At Google, the combined use of statistical language models and the symbolic approaches endorsed by the semantic web is interesting, considering the skepticism that some individuals in leadership positions previously held towards semantic web initiatives (Halevy et al., 2009). Now, several articles from researchers at the company have discussed combining these two approaches (Chari et al., 2020b; Garcez & Lamb, 2020). For years, statistics was the "heart" of data science at these companies. Yet, as Shaw (2015) eloquently puts it, "statistical relationships emerge from the data, but the stable, measurable concepts do not: the concepts are a prerequisite for the existence of the data." Beyond the research, evidence of cooperation between these approaches exists. One merely has to interact with a virtual assistant that has pulled some semantically marked-up structured data or view a knowledge panel that has related some organized information from several sources to convey meaning or knowledge about an entity.

Metadata, Ontologies, and Semantic Technologies

As we wrap up this history, it is worth elaborating on three information science terms that will appear more frequently in the upcoming chapters. These terms are *metadata*, *ontologies*, and *semantic technology*. Metadata, as previously mentioned, are "data about data" (Zeng & Qin, 2016) and allow people and machines to add context to primary data, including timestamps, geolocation, and authorship. The digital data trails produced by machines often contain metadata (just right-click a file and select "properties" to see some examples). Scholars have long described metadata's wide variety of uses (Buckland, 1991; Baca, 2016; Iliadis et al., 2021). These include labeling unique objects (e.g., people, places, things), properties (e.g., colors, height, weight), and their relationships (e.g., familial, organizational, physical), all for different purposes (e.g., descriptive, structural, administrative). Metadata can also link different data types (e.g., formats, locations, domains), thus bridging two other data points.

Metadata are thus helpful for identifying digital traces and connecting widely divergent data that may otherwise have remained non-interoperable (Fidler & Acker, 2016; Mayernik & Acker, 2018). Standardizing this metadata for such linking purposes in larger projects requires what information science refers to as an "ontology." An ontology is a highly regulated set of formal metadata rules, terms, values, and relationships with which different groups of people or machines may serialize, tag, and model their data (Pomerantz, 2015). The purpose of an ontology is to maintain metadata consistency over time and between users (or organizations), thus ensuring that divergent data may cohere for browsing and consumption. The ontologies made from metadata may be instantiated (serialized and visualized) in code and software (e.g., in standardized syntaxes, dashboards, analytics pages). These pieces of code/software are typically known as "semantic technologies" that allow users to curate, browse, share, and refine their data-organizing activities (Fürber, 2016).

According to in-house researchers at internet firms, such technologies are employed on the backend by companies like Google, Microsoft, Amazon, and Facebook to assist with labeling and modeling their vast and diverse troves of data stores (e.g., data about their users and their products). This modeling allegedly allows them to derive "knowledge" from their triangulated data (Noy et al., 2019b, 2019c offer intriguing descriptions of this modeling at internet companies, co-authored by employees from Google, Microsoft, and Facebook). They also play key behind-the-scenes roles in algorithmic media and act as support systems for algorithms that deliver content. According to researchers at Google, algorithms are only a tiny part of a complex digital media system's supporting operations. Thus, there is a vast amount of hidden technical debt in machine learning systems (Sculley et al., 2015; Bender et al., 2021; Iliadis & Acker, 2022). Figure 1.4 represents the relatively small amount of existing algorithmic code (the black box in the center) and the necessary surrounding digital infrastructure for large-scale systems. There are several areas in the infrastructure where metadata, ontologies, and semantic technologies for modeling and tracking play key roles, including data analysis and management.

Today, several conferences are dedicated to these semantic technologies and have attendees that often include representatives from large internet and media companies. These include the Semantics conference, the Knowledge Graph conference, the Connected Data conference, the International Semantic Web Conference, and journals in semantic data modeling and applied computational ontology. A noticeable difference at these events is that some technologies are used in proprietary domains such as for-profit businesses and corporations, while others are in more open and public projects such as those in academia and governments. In the next chapter, we will look at the knowledge graph products of corporate media technology companies.

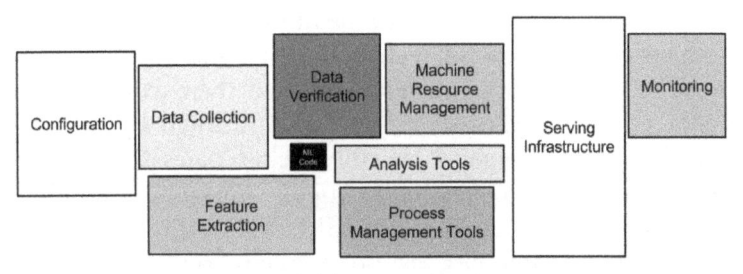

Figure 1.4: Hidden technical debt in machine learning systems

Source: Sculley et al., 2015

Knowledge representation in computing through metadata, ontologies, and semantic technologies (via semantic triples described above) has a clear line leading back to Peirce's ideas on semiotics (Sowa, 1999; Bergman, 2018). Such technologies for labeling, organizing, and tracking data extend early ontology engineering and knowledge representation systems previously discussed (McComb, 2004; Abbas, 2010; Glushko, 2013; Kendall & McGuinness, 2019; Kejriwal et al., 2021). These technologies also have a long and complex history related to web metadata standards, infrastructure, and governance systems (Domingue et al., 2011; DeNardis, 2014), beginning with Berners-Lee's semantic web initiative and W3C (Berners-Lee et al., 2001).

All these technologies are not without problems. As Halavais (2008/2017) notes, the semantic web proposed to extend the web so that computers could interact with data and make inferences. Yet, as critics like Golumbia (2009) have pointed out, such projects are also incredibly monolingual; Golumbia describes this as the "irony" of being offered tools that ask you to forfeit your language. Since these earlier critiques, the web has changed significantly, and semantic tools are, in fact, widely used now in media products in ways that were not present only a decade ago. Still, injustices and sociocultural biases remain regarding unequal knowledge representation, such as what gets included in these knowledge infrastructures and how it is covered.

The next chapter will leave the more extensive history of semantics and semantic technologies behind and focus on how modern companies have adjusted their technologies to take advantage of semantic media through *knowledge graphs* (which depend on the technologies previously discussed). Companies like Apple, Amazon, Alphabet (Google), Microsoft, Tencent, IBM, and Meta (Facebook) use these technologies, as do popular app makers like Airbnb, Pinterest, and Uber. Knowledge graphs are a data-centric approach to storing and working with information.

Data-centric design at the micro level (data and metadata) rather than the meso level (software and databases) allows for greater interoperability between systems. So there has been a gradual shift to this data-centric approach to data management, which researchers have covered. McComb (2018) covers the disadvantages of application-centric computing, and Dourish (2017) discusses the shifting materialities and histories of database formatting and storage.[12] Business leaders and engineers claim that such data-focused modeling approaches reduce the number of necessary applications and databases. Indeed, this seems to be where media systems are heading, particularly concerning the internet-based management of facts and answers.

2

Knowledge Graphs

Semantic media are intimately tied to search engine technologies, and search has drastically changed over the last decade. Media companies now understand that the statistical looking for and matching of keywords is an algorithmic process that doesn't necessarily involve what we could call an *understanding* of those words. The process is more like finding matches and associations of graphical and lexical appearance rather than getting at the underlying meaning. These keywords lead people to pages, and those pages typically are ranked in terms of their importance. But this technique is not the most efficient approach to answering questions.

Since roughly 1998, Google has indexed all web pages on the internet by crawling them and storing their content and location (a Uniform Resource Locator, or URL). Google then uses an algorithmic sorting tool called PageRank (a variation of this is still used today after roughly 20 years, among several other means) to measure the importance of a webpage. PageRank uses a graph algorithm that assesses the quality of links by processing the whole graph topology. The algorithm produces a list of search results based on a user keyword search and how important each page is (Brin & Page, 1998a, 1998b).

Yet, very early on, Google co-founder Sergey Brin focused not only on ranking algorithms to parse unstructured lexical data to create lists of results, he also discussed orchestrating information on the web in an organized manner to capture the *meaning* of specific structured data. In a paper titled "Extracting patterns and relations from the World Wide Web" (Brin, 1999), Brin wonders "if these chunks of information could be extracted from the World Wide Web and integrated into a structured form" and described his goal as being "able to extract structured data from the entire World Wide Web by leveraging on its vastness." This process sounds interestingly like the knowledge panels that Google and other companies use today. Indeed, Google filed a patent way back in 1997, which seems to be the source of the above text from 1999, similarly titled "Extracting patterns and relations from scattered databases such as the World Wide Web." The reference to the web as a "scattered database" is also reminiscent of the semantic web's description of the web as a "web of data."

A ranking of web pages produced in response to a keyword search was the primary way search engines functioned until roughly ten years ago. Around 2012, Google switched the focus of its search products to identifying the meaning of searches rather than just keyword matching. They released several products and updates that would change search dynamics, the most important being the Google Knowledge Graph. According to a Google blog post by Amit Singhal, the former Senior Vice President of Search at Google, the change would switch Google's focus from identifying algorithmic "strings" of content (matching keywords and producing rankings) to understanding the meaning of "things" (Singhal, 2012). This change meant that Google would focus on identifying objects, relations, and processes in the real world, which Google could describe in response to user queries. "The perfect search engine should understand exactly what you mean," Singhal writes. Google would now understand the concept of a search query rather than just the words in the query. In this, Google officially entered the realm of ontology building by trying to define things and their relationships to understand the meaning of entities in the world, after which they could then link information.

Semantic Search

Such a shift would lead to what has been called *semantic search*, which deals with how media companies discern and present meaning about objects and relations to users in response to questions. Kasenchak (2019) describes semantic search as "an attempt to move beyond simple text matching to take into account the context of the search to provide more accurate information retrieval." For example, I may want to know about the mayor of a city or a revolutionary historical figure. Suppose I was to type that person's name into an older search engine that primarily uses keyword matching and ranking. In that case, I may get a list of results from websites that discuss various aspects of that individual's life. Perhaps some would lead to a biography on a website, or maybe the links would lead to a place where I could buy a book about this person. Using semantic search, if I were to conduct the same query, I could instantly view vital biographical details about this individual directly on the search results page, along with a ranked list of results that I may or may not choose. In this example, engineers designed the product to guess what I was looking for and provide facts in the results.

Semantic search thus seeks to improve on things like understanding user intent, such as what the user is trying to know (Battelle, 2006 refers to Google as a "database of intentions") and the contextual meaning of terms. Such technologies provide web products with answers that can help with questions like "What is the closest beach to Da Nang?" or provide relevant and contextual solutions rather than matching them to sites containing only the word string. Or, using another example, if I search for "Best Books of the year," the media product shows a carousel of the best books of the year rather than only links to websites that may have such lists.

Search Engine Optimization (SEO) specialists describe this new era of search well, particularly in SEO articles by Barysevich (2021) and Slawski (2020) in the *Search Engine Journal*. The age is one of so-called "entity-oriented search," or what Balog (2018) describes as "the search paradigm of organizing and accessing information centered around entities, and their attributes and relation-ships" to understand the "meaning" of things. This process allows media companies to disambiguate entities in their search results, allegedly more "intuitively" helping users find the things they are browsing. In straightforward terms, media companies on the internet are now putting *things* first and then information *about* those things second. Concepts of existing things are now the critical object of the search, which attempts to connect other concepts by identifying relations. The job is to identify a term representing the real-world object of a user's search and then provide contextualized information about that object. As Dong et al. (2008) state, semantic search is an application of the semantic web, and that, when compared "with the traditional search engines that focus on the frequency of word appearance, semantic search engines are more likely to try to understand the meanings hidden in retrieved documents and users' queries."

Knowledge Bases

Thus far, we have mentioned the phrase "knowledge graphs" several times in the context of Google's knowledge panels. There is an important distinction between knowledge graphs and knowledge bases, though they are closely related. *Knowledge bases* are effectively large databases that contain facts about the world and have existed for decades. I discussed examples and publications in the last chapter—recall the Cyc project. These knowledge bases are still in use today, and we'll look at how companies like Google use them. *Knowledge graphs* are different from knowledge bases in that they consume incoming data that has been pulled from the web and not only those data that come from a knowledge base. They often pull "external" data into the graph (for example, from other websites marked up with semantic metadata), though companies often use both. Knowledge graphs have become popular with the rise of the industrial-scale web and the desire to "absorb" all the facts scattered across the internet. A critical component for doing this is to use an ontology or schema (we'll look at an example in the next chapter) that web builders can use to tag the facts on their sites. By using knowledge bases and graphs, companies like Google and others can orchestrate facts in their products in "intuitive" ways, reducing the number of times users need to navigate away to other sources.

A pivotal moment in Google's shift to focusing on semantics came in 2010 when it purchased a data management company called Metaweb. Danny Hillis, Veda Hlubinka-Cook, and John Giannandrea founded Metaweb in 2005 and focused on designing knowledge base technology. The company created a knowledge base product called Freebase, an extensive database of facts about the world—Metaweb described it as an "open, shared database of the world's knowledge." *The New York Times* published an article in 2007 titled "Start-up aims for database to automate web searching" (Markoff, 2007). The reporters describe Freebase as "a vast public database intended to be read by computers rather than people, paving the way for a more automated Internet in which machines will routinely share information." The article also calls Freebase "a centralized repository that is more like a digital almanac." Interestingly, the report quotes Hillis saying that the project will help develop "the semantic web—a set of services that will give rise to software agents that automate many functions now performed manually in front of a Web browser." Near the time of its shuttering (Google began merging Freebase with Wikidata in 2015), Freebase consisted of 44 million topics and 2.4 billion facts (one can use the Internet Archive's Wayback Machine to see the tally on the original Freebase website).

Google released a statement about the Freebase acquisition in their official blog on July 16, 2010, titled "Deeper understanding with Metaweb" (Menzel, 2010). The blog read in part: "The web isn't merely words—it's information about things in the real world, and understanding the relationships [...] Today, we've acquired Metaweb, a company that maintains an open database of things in the world." The blog provided examples, stating users can now search for "Barack Obama's birthday" and see the answer right away, or "events in San Jose" and receive a list of events. "We can offer this kind of experience because we understand facts about real people and real events out in the world," the statement said. It describes Freebase as consisting of facts about "movies, books, TV shows, celebrities, locations, companies and more." Not long after the Metaweb acquisition, Google changed the name of its "Search" division to "Knowledge" (Arrington, 2011).

Some scholars have conducted work that analyzes the Freebase and Google knowledge bases. In "OK Google, what is your ontology? Or: Exploring Freebase classification to understand Google's Knowledge Graph," Chah (2018) "reconstructs the Freebase data dumps to understand the underlying ontology behind Google's semantic search feature." He indicates that these data included 1.9 billion RDF triples (facts represented as subjects, predicates, and objects like I described in the previous chapter). The study focused on Google to "provide a glimpse into the proprietary blackbox Knowledge Graph" (Chah, 2017 provides further information on this project). Chah notes that "Freebase can also serve as a gateway to other structured datasets, such as DBpedia, Wikidata, and YAGO." Interestingly, when I did a Google search for "Niel Chah" recently, the knowledge panel returned information about the University of Toronto where Niel went to school, but no information about Niel, sadly.

There are other knowledge bases besides Freebase, which also store facts as semantic triples (among additional information). Some of these other knowledge bases include Wikidata (a combination of the words "Wikipedia" and "data"), DBpedia (a combination of the words "database" and "Wikipedia"), YAGO (which stands for "Yet Another Great Ontology"), and Cyc (short for "encyclopedia," and the longest-running among the knowledge bases).

Wikidata engineers describe it as a "free knowledge base with 95,913,094 data items that anyone can edit," acting "as central storage for the structured data of its Wikimedia sister projects including Wikipedia, Wikivoyage, Wiktionary, Wikisource, and others" (Vrandečić, 2012; Vrandečić & Krötzsch, 2014). DBpedia "constitutes the main resource of Linked Open Data on the Web containing more than 228 million entities" and "contains factual data from articles and infoboxes of the English Wikipedia" (the original paper is Auer et al., 2007); DBpedia is also crowd-sourced. YAGO "is a large knowledge base with general knowledge about people, cities, countries, movies, and organizations," contains "more than 50 million entities and 2 billion facts," and combines data from Wikidata, Schema.org, and WordNet (Suchanek et al., 2007 offers the original description). Cyc's knowledge base "includes more than 40,000 predicates, millions of collections and concepts, and more than 25 million axioms" and trillions of axioms about "real-world knowledge" (Lenat et al., 1985, 1990; Lenat, 1995 are the original works about the project).

Each of these knowledge bases stores its facts in the form of semantic triples (subjects, predicates, objects). Färber et al. (2015, 2018) compare DBpedia, Freebase, Cyc, Wikidata, and YAGO; table 2.1 compares the five knowledge bases and lists the number of their triples, classes, relations, predicates, entities, instances, and other information as of 2015. Another study similarly found that, in terms of assertions of facts, DBpedia contained over 850 million, Cyc 2 million, Wikidata 730 million, and YAGO 479 million (Heist et al., 2020). The number of facts contained in these knowledge bases is not insignificant. Google now includes results from several of these in its Knowledge Graph, including Freebase (after it acquired the company) and Wikidata—we will take a more in-depth look at Wikidata in chapter 4. Other than simply presenting facts, these knowledge bases are used by large internet companies when they must perform entity resolution tasks to combine data and erase duplicates from different sources (Christophides et al., 2015). For example, suppose there is data about "Harriet Tubman" serialized in each knowledge base or other sources under different codes. In that case, a company's knowledge graph can reconcile those codes into one entity named "Harriet Tubman."

Table 2.1: Quantities in five knowledge bases

	DBpedia	Freebase	Opencyc	Wikidata	YAGO
Number of triples	411 885 960	3 124 791 156	2 412 520	748 530 833	1 001 461 792
Number of classes	736	53 092	116 822	302 280	569 751
Number of relations	58 776	70 902	18 028	1874	106
Unique predicates	60 231	784 977	165	4839	88 736
Number of entities	4 298 433	49 947 799	41 029	18 697 897	5 130 031
Number of instances	20 764 283	115 880 761	242 383	142 213 806	12 291 250
Avg. number of entities per class	5840.3	940.8	0.35	61.9	9
Unique subjects without blank nodes	31 391 413	125 144 313	239 264	142 213 806	331 806 927
Number of blank nodes	0	0	21 833	64 348	0
Unique non-literals in object position	83 284 634	189 466 866	423 432	101 745 685	17 438 196
Unique literals in object position	161 398 382	1 782 723 759	1 081 818	308 144 682	682 313 508

Source: Färber et al., 2018

Knowledge Graphs

Now that we've covered some detail about knowledge bases, it's time to understand knowledge graphs better. Before we move on to Google's Knowledge Graph, it might be helpful to articulate a definition of what exactly knowledge graphs are. The term "knowledge graphs" is a relatively new invention, thanks to industrial-scale knowledge graphs such as Google's Knowledge Graph and Amazon's Product Graph. Knowledge graphs are organized data models about "things in the world" that enable sharing of heterogeneous data resources that conform to a model. According to Kejriwal et al. (2021), knowledge graphs are examples of using technology (like metadata, ontologies, and semantic technologies) "for representing (and reasoning over) data that can be semistructured and web scale in origin." For example, many websites or researchers could agree to use the same knowledge graph for organizing their information (meaning, they might agree on using the same types of metadata terms, vocabulary, and ontological organization). This organizing would increase their data interoperability once the agreed-upon semantics harmonize through the application of uniform nomenclature. Knowledge graphs can be open and public or closed and proprietary, and companies like Google have been developing them since at least 2012 to help their organization retrieve and process information. Different data types can feed the knowledge graph, coming from several sources. If you have ever seen a panel on Google that relays information about a person, place, or thing, you have interacted with a knowledge graph product.

Hogan et al. (2021) offer a detailed history of knowledge graphs, referring to them as "a graph of data intended to accumulate and convey knowledge of the real world, whose nodes represent entities of interest and whose edges represent potentially different relations between these entities." The article describes some critical distinctions in knowledge graph research, including the differences between implicit and explicit knowledge, deductive and inductive reasoning, and open vs. enterprise knowledge graphs, among other areas. Gutiérrez and Sequeda (2020, 2021) also offer a history of the knowledge graph's main ideas, including accounts of the graphical representation of knowledge, reasoning automation, space searching, information retrieval of unstructured sources, and language systems for data. Sequeda and Lassila (2021) provide a history of knowledge graphs and describe them from the beginning as semantic web and RDF technologies. The authors define knowledge graphs as "integrating knowledge and data at scale where the real-world concepts and relationships are first class citizens." Knowledge graphs are "a collection of real-world concepts (i.e., nodes) and relationships (i.e., edges) in the form of a graph used to link and integrate data coming from diverse sources."

One can argue that "knowledge graphs" are simply the latest "turn" in the history of a series of semantic technologies that began with the "semantic web," through to "linked data," and now to "knowledge graphs." There may be a good reason that "knowledge graphs" are beginning to be used by more casual internet users in a way that the other branded projects never were. Allemang et al. (2020) write that, around 2012, "Google felt that the use of the name Knowledge Graph, instead of something that seemed more esoteric like Semantic Web, would make it easier for people to understand the basic concept." Instead of a "Web of Semantics, they would prefer to call it a Graph of Knowledge." Even though the technologies are rooted in the same semantic tradition, now they are used by massive media technology companies like Google, Amazon, Facebook, and Microsoft. So, it is unsurprising that, as those companies are now using these technologies, there should also be a rebranding.

The idea of semantic media attracted large internet companies even before the Google announcement. Before Google popularized the term and the technologies in public, a team of researchers from Yahoo published a paper titled "A web of concepts" (Dalvi et al., 2009). The abstract clearly describes the coming change in semantic media technologies and comments on the shift from thinking about media in terms of lists of blue links to rich details about things in the world curated through metadata orchestration. It reads:

> We make the case for developing a web of concepts by starting with the current view of web (comprised of hyperlinked pages, or documents, each seen as a bag of words), extracting concept-centric metadata, and stitching it together to create a semantically rich aggregate view of all the information available on the web for each concept instance.

The phrase "a semantically rich aggregate view of all the information available on the web for each concept instance" is an elegant and accurate way to describe the then-emerging media technologies of this new era. The authors state that building such a concept graph on a web scale would be challenging. Still, the payoff would be enormous and lead to a paradigm shift in media products that could then understand and reason with knowledge about the world. The paper includes references to the semantic web ("our goals are closely related to the semantic web, and we see the two approaches as synergistic"). It also describes "using semantic web terminology." The authors state that their emphasis is on interpreting web data to provide richer products and that the semantic web empowers "authors to publish content in a more interpretable form."

Papers like the one authored by the Yahoo researchers represent the beginning of the shift to semantic media. They also represent the moment when the original dream of the semantic web began to shift from being a primarily free and open way of sharing knowledge to one where such knowledge is constructed and offered by large internet companies. A moment where one might interpret the semantic web's original democratic dream as having been debased by for-profit companies like Yahoo. The idea became something like: "We build our knowledge bases via web semantics, and we will also take all that rich semantic data that you all have curated in your websites, sucking it up into our systems, which can then represent your data along with ours in our products." The Yahoo paper describes this information extraction as pulling structured data from web sources, linking it by mapping the identified entities and relationships, and categorizing all entities' information.

Major news about the use, extent, and pervasiveness of knowledge graphs at media technology companies came in 2019 with the publication of a slightly unusual, co-authored article. In an article titled "Industry-scale knowledge graphs: Lessons and challenges" (Noy et al., 2019b, 2019c)—co-authored by employees from Google, Microsoft, IBM, Facebook, and eBay (all traditionally commercial competitors in several domains)—the co-authors describe the knowledge graphs at their companies (without giving away any crucial secrets), providing information about their data models, sizes of their graphs, and their developmental stages (table 2.2). Each knowledge graph contains entities and relations (triples), millions or billions of facts, and all are used actively in the media technology products released by the companies. The article appears based on an "Enterprise-scale knowledge graphs" panel held the previous year during the 17th International Semantic Web Conference, which included the same representatives from the same companies (Gao et al., 2018). Let us now turn to Google's Knowledge Graph before exploring those used by a few other companies and industries.

Table 2.2: Media technology companies' knowledge graphs

	Data model	Size of the graph	Development stage
Microsoft	The types of entities, relations, and attributes in the graph are defined in an ontology.	2 billion primary entities, 55 billion facts	Actively used in products
Google	Strongly typed entities, relations with domain and range inference	1 billion entities, 70 billion assertions	Actively used in products
Facebook	All of the attributes and relations are structured and strongly typed, and optionally indexed to enable efficient retrieval, search, and traversal.	50 million primary entities, 500 million assertions	Actively used in products
eBay	Entities and relation, well-structured and strongly typed	Expect around 100 million products, >1 billion triples	Early stages of development and deployment
IBM	Entities and relations with evidence informationassociated with them.	Various sizes. Proven on scales documents >100 million, relationships >5 billion, entities >100 million	Actively used in products and by clients

Source: Noy et al., 2019c

Google's Knowledge Graph

Noy et al. (2019b, 2019c) describe Google's Knowledge Graph as "a long-term, stable source of class and entity identity that many Google products and features use behind the scenes" and state that it "helps Google products interpret user requests as references to concepts in the world of the user." The authors also describe how the Google Knowledge Graph helps with actions: it "recognizes that certain kinds of interactions can take place with different entities." For example, a search for "'Russian Tea Room' provides a button to make a reservation, while a query for 'Rita Ora' provides links to her music on various music services." The Google Knowledge Graph contains roughly 1 billion entities and 70 billion assertions.

After Google released its Knowledge Graph in 2012 (the blog post announcement was titled "Introducing the Knowledge Graph: things, not strings"), search fundamentally changed at the company (Singhal, 2012). The post released by Singhal describes how the Knowledge Graph "enables you to search for things, people or places that Google knows about [...] and instantly get information that's relevant to your query." It says that this is "a critical first step towards building the next generation of search, which taps into the collective intelligence of the web and understands the world a bit more like people do." The post seemed to say that Google was now concerned with understanding common sense, echoing the original aspirations of the original ontology engineering researchers from the 1980s.

The following year, as Haider and Sundin (2019) have shown, Google updated its algorithms for search in 2013 via the project Hummingbird, which focused on things like context and meaning rather than only keywords. Hummingbird was the most significant upgrade to Google search since the company's beginnings and increased Google's commitment to semantic search. This approach links to semantic web initiatives discussed earlier. Since roughly 2001, websites and apps began using semantic metadata to mark up their content, and Google became interested in retrieving those underlying semantics to assist with the search. Such a focus would also help with voice search and conversational media that provide contextual answers. Google search could now look for things even if the search terms didn't match exactly; the product could understand "place" as the user wanting to know about a "restaurant" if the user searched the phrase "place to eat," for example.

For more evidence of this shift, one can merely look at patents filed by Google, as those in the SEO community—including Slawski (2013a, 2013b, 2014, 2018a, 2018b) in a series of online articles over the last decade—have done. Google's interest in semantic markup, facts, and contextual search can be detected as far back as a 2006 patent titled "Browseable fact repository" (Hogue & Betz, 2006)—the abstract appears below:

> A fact repository supports searches of facts relevant to search queries comprising keywords and phrases. A service engine retrieves the objects that are associated with facts relevant to the query. The objects are displayed on a search results page. Each object is displayed with selection of the facts associated with the object. The selected facts are ordered according to their relevance to the query.

A 2012 patent, released the same year as the Knowledge Graph, is titled "Providing knowledge panels with search results" (Henry, 2012). The abstract reads, in part, that search queries identify a factual entity. Then, content would be displayed "in a knowledge panel for the factual entity," including data from different sources. These patents clearly describe how Google would take facts from several sources, including internal databases and external websites, and then orchestrate that information in its knowledge panels.

After releasing the Knowledge Graph in 2012 and Hummingbird in 2013, Google published several semantic search and knowledge graphs documents. In 2014, the company issued a patent titled "Knowledge base completion via search-based question answering" (West et al., 2014). It describes "a way to leverage existing Web-search-based question-answering technology to fill in the gaps in knowledge bases in a targeted way," including knowledge bases such as YAGO and Freebase. A similar-sounding patent, titled "Question answering to populate knowledge base" (Gupta et al., 2014), was also released and shows clear images of the connections between subjects, predicates, and objects in their data modeling of a "knowledge" database. Figure 2.1 shows an example scenario involving information relevant to George Washington (notice the triples present in the graph).

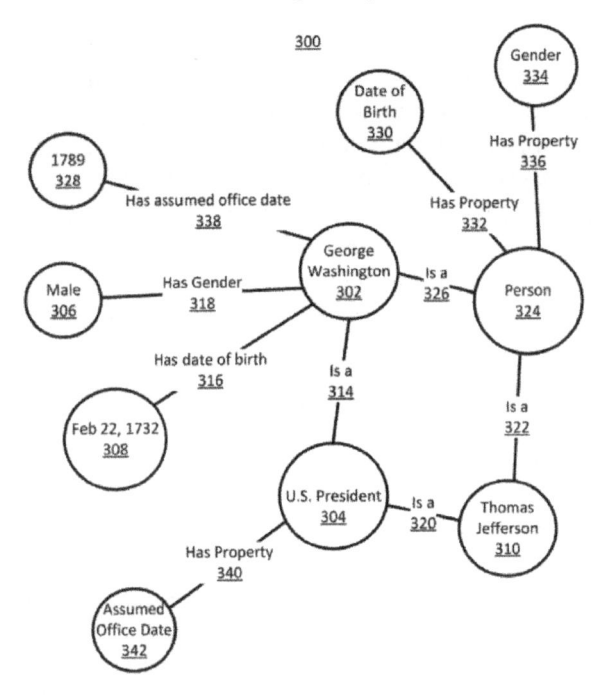

Figure 2.1: "Question Answering to Populate Knowledge Base"

Source: Gupta et al., 2014

In 2014, Google also released a patent titled "Entity identification model training" (Gubin et al., 2014) which discusses how Google will identify entities in searches (things like people and places) and then will pull up information related to those things. A patent from 2017, titled "Predicting intent of a search for a particular context" (Lim et al., 2017), describes how a "computing system adjusts, based on the intent, at least a particular portion of search results obtained from the search using the search query by emphasizing information that satisfies the intent." Google focuses on these areas (knowledge and intent) because they know that people use search engines for different reasons, including navigating, getting information, and making transactions (Hernández et al., 2012). Each of these is also sensitive to time. There are other patents about how the Google Knowledge Graph updates itself and extracts entities to populate it and patents for creating semantic dependency trees that can identify objects and subjects and the actions the user wants to take based on sentence terms. These types of changes over the last few years coincided with the appearance of Google's RankBrain algorithm update in 2016, which is an extension of Hummingbird.

After almost a decade of Knowledge Graph growth, Danny Sullivan, Google's Public Liaison for Search, released a blog post titled "A reintroduction to our Knowledge Graph and knowledge panels" (Sullivan, 2020). In the post, Sullivan remarks that "Google's Knowledge Graph has amassed over 500 billion facts about five billion entities—people, places and things." Regarding inaccuracies in the knowledge panels, Sullivan writes that they can "occasionally happen" and that Google has "automatic systems that gather facts for the Knowledge Graph" and "automatic systems designed to prevent inaccuracies from appearing." But he also says that the systems are not perfect and that that is why Google accepts reports and feedback.

Some information in Google's Knowledge Graph comes from authoritative and sometimes even intelligence sources, such as the Central Intelligence Agency's World Factbook. Google released a post in 2020 titled "Our latest investments in information quality in search and news" (Nayak, 2020). It describes knowledge panels as providing "quick access to the facts from sources across the web" and that Google has "deepened our partnerships with government agencies, health organizations and Wikipedia to ensure reliable, accurate information is available, and protect against potential vandalism." The post discusses sourcing data from and working with health authorities during the COVID-19 pandemic and non-partisan organizations during elections. The data comes from hundreds of sources, and they admit that errors or vandalism within Wikipedia can slip through to the knowledge graph.

Google offers an application programming interface (API) for its Knowledge Graph Search to find entities in the graph and explore it. Still, as of this writing, it is not meant to support other apps and devices in the same way that an API from, say, Google Maps can. The examples provided by Google of what users can do with the Graph Search API include finding ranked lists of entities that match search criteria, autocompleting entities in a search bar, and organizing content using the graph's entities.

Critiques of Google's Knowledge Graph

Among the more visible aspects of web semantics, several studies have examined the semantic products of platforms such as knowledge graphs (Kejriwal et al., 2021). Vang (2013) examines Google's position as a semantic entity modeler as evidenced through its Knowledge Graph product, arguing that Google's knowledge panels work to monopolize its hold on information, keeping users on Google's pages. Monea (2016) critically dissects modern knowledge databases, including Google's Knowledge Graph and its expression of difference, articulating a latent logic of representation that renders the feature unable to discern difference meaningfully. Uyar and Aliyu (2015) evaluate Google's Knowledge Graph and Bing's Satori; after conducting a series of searches, Uyar and Aliyu claim that semantic search systems limit the conceptual complexity permitted within each system.

Other researchers have documented that Google results push out smaller companies and organizations that depend on visitors interacting directly with their products and that Google has "structural tendencies towards monopoly" (Rieder & Sire, 2014). Like its knowledge panels, Google's web-based products often provide people with direct answers to their queries and offer them opportunities to take specific actions immediately, rather than serve as an engine to direct readers to other sources.

Facebook's Graphs

As mentioned previously, Google is not the only company engaging with and building knowledge graphs. Facebook's knowledge graph currently contains 50 million entities and 500 million assertions and "focuses on the most socially relevant entities, such as those that are most commonly discussed by its users: celebrities, places, movies, and music" (Noy et al. 2019b, 2019c).

There are several other ways that semantics play a role in Facebook's graphs. Facebook's Open Graph protocol was launched in 2010, putting Facebook slightly ahead of Google in publicly acknowledging the use of semantics in its knowledge graph products. It is also how Facebook connects to entities outside of Facebook and then represents them internally, as when users log into services and apps using Facebook or when websites implement Facebook extensions in their content. The Open Graph brings these distributed and "external" entities and actions into the central Facebook graph.

Several Facebook products that have appeared over the years or are currently still used interact with or contribute to the graph. These items include Facebook's "like" function, which creates edges (predicates) between objects and subjects (for example, the semantic triple "Isabel likes [Italian restaurant]" can be represented in the graph). Gerlitz and Helmond (2013) describe how the Open Graph connects to Facebook "likes" and how it creates infrastructure to allow Facebook features to be "distributed across the web" while centralizing them at Facebook with "the processing of user data." Bucher (2021) provides an account of Facebook's Open Graph and its Graph API—the primary way developers can pull data from and interact with the Facebook social graph. Bucher describes the Open Graph as "a way of building a semantic map of the internet, by offering a standardized means for external websites to integrate and exchange data with Facebook using simple markup languages and tags." Halavais (2008/2017) describes Open Graph as allowing "for structured filtering of information found within Facebook," and Karppi (2018) explains how the Open Graph expresses "a range of more specific coded actions toward particular objects, such as reading and watching" all "without leaving the Facebook interface." The Open Graph website (see ogp.me) states that it "enables any web page to become a rich object in a social graph. For instance, this is used on Facebook to allow any web page to have the same functionality as any other object on Facebook."

Open Graph is like the previous RDF data model (semantic triples), which came out of early semantic web initiatives. In an article titled "One trillion edges: Graph processing at Facebook-scale," Facebook researchers state that the Open Graph "allows application developers to connect objects in their applications with real-world actions (such as user X is listening to song Y)." They write that the triples in "these real world graphs" are "at the scale of hundreds of billions or even a trillion edges" (Ching et al., 2015). Kaldrack and Röhle (2014) state that "the increasing spread of the underlying Open Graph protocol is establishing new classification schemata on the web" and that following "the RDF specification formulated by the World Wide Web Consortium, Open Graph merges the model of network analysis with semantic categorization." Other researchers at Facebook describe the Open Graph as enabling "any web page to become a rich object in a social graph" (Haugen, 2010). Haugen (2010) states that, at the time, there was "not a single technology which provides enough information to richly represent any web page within the social graph."

Facebook Graph Search, introduced in 2013, was a semantic search engine based on the graph, allowing regular users and researchers to begin searching for specific things on Facebook. An example of this type of search would be "My friends who listen to Rage Against the Machine who live in New York City." Facebook describes the product as "giving people the tools to map out their relationships with the people and things they care about" including "already more than a billion people, more than 240 billion photos and more than a trillion connections" (Stocky & Rasmussen, 2013). The announcement stated that web search "is designed to take a set of keywords (for example: 'hip hop') and provide the best possible results that match those keywords." Graph search, instead, can "combine phrases (for example: 'my friends in New York who like Jay-Z') to get that set of people, places, photos or other content that's been shared on Facebook." A *TechCrunch* article covered the announcement and describes how the new feature allows one to search for things like "Who are my friends that live in San Francisco?" (Olanoff et al., 2013).

Another Facebook post from around the time Graph Search was released describes the Open Graph in terms of entities. The post states that an entity graph would connect people and their interests in places and things, which themselves can take graph form as nodes and edges. The "entities engineering team at Facebook" is described as "charged with building, cleaning, and understanding

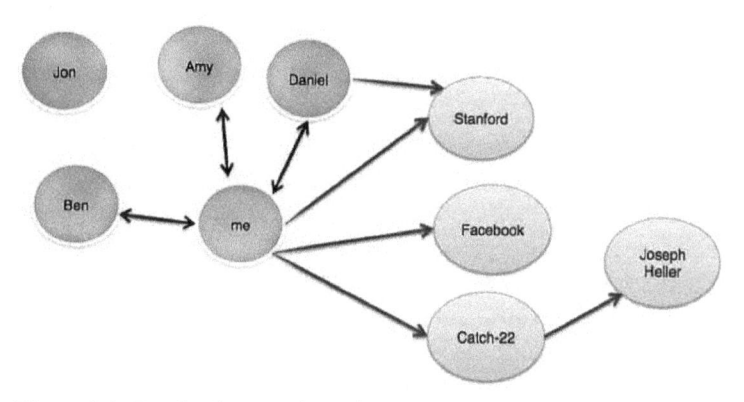

Figure 2.2: Facebook entity knowledge representation

Source: Sun, 2013

this graph" to "bring structure and meaning to data," and also states that they use WordNet to help clean up the search terms (Sun, 2013). Figure 2.2 shows an example of the entities graph from the Facebook team; it displays people connected to a primary user who connects to a school, a book, etc. Another Facebook engineering post clearly describes the graph in terms of semantic triples (entities and relationships) represented in the metadata (Sankar et al., 2013):

> The entities are the nodes and the relationships are the edges. One way to think of this is if the graph were represented by language, the nodes would be the nouns and the edges would be the verbs. Every user, page, place, photo, post, etc. are nodes in this graph. Edges between nodes represent friendships, check-ins, tags, relationships, ownership, attributes, etc. Both nodes and edges have metadata associated with them. For example, the node corresponding to me will have my name, my birthday, etc. and the node corresponding to the Page Breville will have its title and description as metadata.

There are semantic web vocabularies such as Friend of a Friend (Graves et al., 2007; Brickley & Miller, 2014) specifically designed to mark up social entities and their relationships. Facebook's Open Graph certainly took advantage of these ideas from the semantic web. Though Open Graph is still active, Graph Search was shuttered to the public beginning in 2014 and concluded by 2019 for what one can assume were obvious privacy issues. Yet, the underlying technology that enables it is still active and used on Facebook. Vaidhyanathan (2018) critiques Open Graph, stating that its actions "become part of the larger social graph and thus useful for profiling and targeting" and that "the use of tracking cookies that it implants in users' web browsers, is able to gather immense amounts of personal data from people who hardly ever log in to their Facebook accounts. Basically, there is no way to opt out fully from Facebook's ability to track you."

Amazon's Graphs

Several other large internet companies use graphs to organize "knowledge" about things in their products. Amazon has something called the Amazon Product Graph that manages information about products in the way that Google does the same for general knowledge and that Facebook does with knowledge about contemporary and popular cultural artifacts and social relations. Amazon's Product Knowledge Graph contains media subdomain graphs, including the Media Knowledge Graph (information about books, music, movies, podcasts, etc.), the Retail Knowledge Graph, and web knowledge extraction, including information from brands and companies on the web. The Media Knowledge Graph integrates the metadata from several databases that already use semantic technologies. In contrast, the Retail Knowledge Graph attempts to produce a structure from the unstructured natural language of retail information.

Luna Dong, the former Senior Principal Scientist at Amazon, has described the processes involved in creating these graphs in several places and has touched on the nature of the Product Knowledge Graph as "a set of triples in the form of (subject, predicate, object)" (Dong et al., 2020). Representatives from Amazon have attended the Knowledge Graph conference. They have presented papers that describe Amazon graphs and their relationships to the RDF data model and the semantic web and experiments with things like Freebase. Such representatives included Brad Bebee, product and engineering lead for Amazon Neptune, and Subhabrata Mukherjee, machine learning scientist at Amazon (Columbia SPS, 2019a, 2019b).

Microsoft's Graphs

Microsoft has several knowledge graph-like products, including Bing's Satori, Academic Graph, and LinkedIn

Graph. Their knowledge graphs contain 2 billion entities and 55 billion facts (Noy et al., 2019b, 2019c).

Microsoft researchers state that Satori, the Bing knowledge graph, includes "information about the world and powers question answering on Bing. It contains entities such as people, places, things, organizations, locations, and so on, as well as the actions that a user might take"—it is stated that "its aim is to contain general knowledge about the entire world" (Noy et al., 2019b, 2019c). Satori is a Japanese Buddhist term for "understanding." The company announced the product not long after Google announced its Knowledge Graph, in 2013. In a blog post introducing Satori, the company writes, "we believe that search should be more than a collection of blue links pointing to pages around the web. We believe search should also be a reflection of the actual world" and that the technology was "designed to develop deep understanding of the world around us not only as a collection of entities (people, places and things) but also the relationships between those entities" (Qian, 2013). The post goes on: "Over time, Satori will continue growing to encompass billions of entities and relationships, providing searchers with a more useful model of the digital and physical world." *Ars Technica* released an article from the same period titled "How Google and Microsoft taught search to 'understand' the web" (Gallagher, 2012). The reporting notes that Satori helps Bing by creating "a structured database of the 'nouns' of the Internet: people, places, things, and the relationships between them all." Like Google and Facebook's APIs, Microsoft has released a Bing Entity Search API that "sends a search query to Bing and gets results that include entities and places" and will enable users to do real-time search suggestions and entity disambiguation and to find places.

There is clear evidence that Microsoft has sought to connect its semantic technologies in their products to produce specific actions (think of some of the Bing carousels and results for trip suggestions discussed in the introduction). A year before the Satori announcement, researchers from Microsoft released a paper in 2012 titled "Active objects: Actions for entity-centric search," which describes "an entity-centric search experience [...] in which entity-bearing queries are paired with actions that can be performed on the entities" (Lin et al., 2012). The example they provide shows that when a user searches for a term like "flashlight," the results can include various pieces of orchestrated information that allow users to conduct "reading reviews, watching demo videos, and finding the best price." They describe how users search for entities and how their intentions differ depending on whether they are instructional, navigational, or transactional (Broder, 2002). Figure 2.3 shows how this process occurs (the figure describes a user as having an intent to plan a trip or to get in shape and then how Microsoft will organize actions for them to take).

Companies are also producing graphs based on the world's research. Microsoft's Academic Graph is

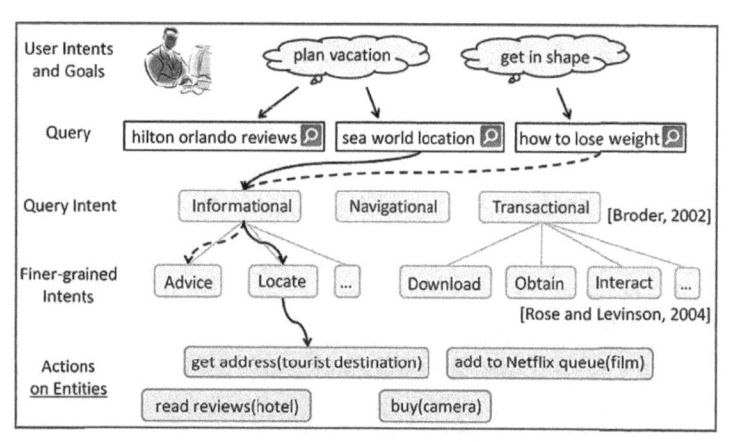

Figure 2.3: Intentional search for entities on Bing from Microsoft

Source: Lin et al., 2012. Active objects: Actions for entity-centric search. In *Proceedings of the 21st International Conference on World Wide Web.* Courtesy of the International World Wide Web Conference Committee (IW3C2)

described as "a large RDF data set with over eight billion triples with information about scientific publications and related entities, such as authors, institutions, journals, and fields of study" (Färber, 2019). The graph contains over 238 million publications, 151 million authors, 1 billion references, and 234 million citations, among other data. This information, plus the LinkedIn graph, provides Microsoft with billions of entities and relationships identified in products, including new analytics the company has developed around workplace technologies (see the recently launched Project Cortex). Microsoft has been developing a knowledge base called Probase since 2010. Probase has recently benefitted from their Concept Graph project, which collects over 5 million concepts, 12 million instances, and 85 million relations from the web using machine learning. The *TechCrunch* article "Microsoft strives to give computers common sense with Concept Graph" (Mannes, 2016) describes the project. According to research by Microsoft, Probase is currently the most extensive knowledge base around— their researchers document it in papers like "Microsoft Concept Graph: Mining semantic concepts for short text understanding" (Ji et al., 2019).

Airbnb, Uber, Netflix, Pinterest, and Spotify Graphs

Media technology companies not quite as large as Google, Facebook, Amazon, and Microsoft also use knowledge graphs in their products. Google's product and the others are broader knowledge graphs that aim to cover "knowledge." These smaller graphs tend to be domain-specific, focusing on a particular area. Researchers from Pinterest have described how "the company adopted Semantic Web technologies to create a knowledge graph that aims to represent the vast amount of content and users on Pinterest, to help both content recommendation and ads targeting" (Gonçalves et al., 2019). These technologies include OWL, which engineers used to create the Pinterest Taxonomy and the Pinterest Taste Graph (the name of Pinterest's knowledge graph). The company hosted a Pinterest Knowledge Graph Summit in 2020. Posts on the Pinterest engineering blog describe using RDF and semantic data models to work with their data: "Taxonomy is a methodology that classifies entities and defines the hierarchical relationship among them. It's widely used as a knowledge management system in the industry, and has proven success in improving the accuracy of the machine learning models in search, user-behavior modeling, and classification tasks" (Cui & Shrouty, 2020). They also use machine learning techniques to classify and map their 200 billion pins in their "interest taxonomy" (Li, 2019).

According to the Netflix Tech Blog, Netflix uses a knowledge graph to orchestrate its content about genres, movies, documentaries, and television shows (Dye et al., 2020). Airbnb uses an RDF-based knowledge graph to organize data for food and drink, entertainment and activities, and landmarks and points of interest (Chang, 2018; Wei & Liao, 2019). The company also had its researchers present at the Knowledge Graph conference and posted jobs in the knowledge graph area. Eriksson et al. (2019) write that Spotify requires "information residing 'outside' and then 'pulled into' Spotify's data infrastructure" and that it is "of utmost importance [...] Linked data (as well as similar concepts around the semantic web) have been a trend in a number of public and commercial domains for more than a decade." Ikea uses ontologies and knowledge graphs, has a Lead Ontologist job position, and is an active semantic web practitioner. They have presented at conferences like Connected Data, which semantic web researchers attend. Yahoo has a knowledge graph (Ni et al., 2020), Electronic Arts has a taxonomist, and IBM has a knowledge graph (Aggarwal et al., 2017). Even the United Nations has discussed using knowledge graphs for social good, including human trafficking (Kejriwal &

Szekely, 2017). The Knowledge Graphs for Social Good website describes this work, and Hogenhout (2021) offers a framework for ethical AI at the United Nations.

News and Journalism Graphs

News and journalism outlets also take advantage of knowledge graphs; sometimes, this is done on the backend to support information search and retrieval for reporters and administrators when categorizing and organizing stories. This process also helps sort through large amounts of information in digital investigative reporting. The BBC uses ontologies and semantic technologies derived from the semantic web to support its knowledge infrastructures (Liu et al., 2014; Mikroyannidi et al., 2016). The Organized Crime and Corruption Reporting Project (OCCRP) uses a data platform called Aleph, which resembles a knowledge graph like Google's. The piece "Things, not strings: Knowledge graphs for investigative reporting" and others (Lindenberg, 2020a, 2020b) describe these and comment on the OCCRP's data platform, which can track nouns and "things" as well as verbs that act as the links between things.

Organizations such as *The New York Times* use knowledge graphs to organize metadata about stories for reporters and readers, and scholars have written on graph integration of structured, semistructured, and unstructured data for data journalism, and often discuss semantic and RDF tools to process the data (Anadiotis et al., 2022). Recently, there have been attempts to create a new type of trusted knowledge base that uses machine learning to track information from traditional knowledge base projects and connect it to web content with structured data (Dong et al., 2014). Other projects, such as Enslaved: Peoples of the Historical Slave Trade (enslaved.org), have used knowledge graphs for "building a robust, open-source architecture to discover, connect, and visualize 600,000 (and growing) people records and 5 million data points" (see the *Journal of Slavery and Data Preservation* which publishes material from the project). The project uses linked data and Wikibase and is "a space for disseminating best practices for data collection, metadata standards, ontology controlled vocabularies, and workflows."

The semantic web technologies that appeared decades ago (discussed in the first chapter) are in all the above domains. They are within popular media products that people interact with every day and shape how knowledge disseminates on the internet. What should concern us is the proprietary and obscured nature of many of the knowledge graphs; the companies discussed above do not make these graphs entirely available, so it is tough for researchers to analyze and understand the knowledge that they contain. The closest thing many researchers can do is analyze the open knowledge bases that exist, along with any public schema languages and ontologies used for marking up data. Some researchers may attempt to reverse engineer these (Gehl, 2014), though doing so would run against company policies. In the following chapters, I provide case studies of these open and available technologies.

3

One Schema to Rule them All

The Tower of Babel is a biblical origin myth (Genesis 11:1–9) explaining why people speak different languages worldwide. God saw the people—a single, monolinguistic unit—and observed their plan to stop and build a city with a great tower to honor themselves (other interpretations suggest they did so to reach heaven, avoid another flood, etc.). God also saw this as blasphemy, and decided to confuse the peoples' speech by separating it into different groups, thus preventing their work on the tower due to lack of communication. Eventually, the people dispersed, scattered across the world and speaking many languages.

Like many growing disciplines, problematic issues in ontology engineering result from a perennial problem—typically, this is referred to as "the Tower of Babel problem" (Smith, 2004; Blass et al., 2007; Arp et al., 2015; Iliadis, 2019). The Tower of Babel problem (ToB) states that new terms develop each time a new ontology is made that represents an ever-changing language. Such practices thus complicate applied ontology building, which aims to produce semantically robust ontologies that can last over time. Sometimes a group of data can be paired to share the same language. Yet, in many cases, data that exist in different domains can be blocked from each other due to labeling differences. In other words, the definitions and relations described in the metadata do not cohere. The ToB problem frustrates ontologists because it constantly introduces new issues that ontology engineering needs to resolve. Each new category and relation from a different domain threaten to undermine an ontology predicated on the heterogeneity of the labels and data structure.

Schemas

Pulling together data from different sources requires an organized metadata vocabulary (ontology), also informally known as a "schema." There are some minor differences between schemas and ontologies. Generally, schemas are simpler versions of ontologies and have a primarily relational structure, whereas ontologies are more expressive, are operation- and logic-based, and have more complex structures. They can both be forms of knowledge representation using a controlled metadata vocabulary, and in this, they are similar. Schemas are general ontologies that can be used to label, mark up, and tag data uniformly, which can then be "pulled" into a knowledge graph as sources—schemas and knowledge graphs thus go hand in hand. This chapter will present a case study of one of the most widely used schemas on the internet today.

Historically, several industry-specific metadata initiatives have facilitated structured data modeling for the web, including in commerce, publishing, and social media domains (Guns, 2013). The markup produced by these initiatives allows web developers to "wrap" information on the web to provide machine-readable signals for advertisers and user-facing content on apps and websites (Amerland, 2013). Thus, the markup assists with information search and retrieval (e.g., surfacing specific facts about people, places, and products). Where such efforts were once fragmented across industries producing sometimes overlapping, nonstandard, and kludgy structured data models (McCarthy, 2017), today this landscape is changing with the appearance of globally coordinated efforts to create a universal structured data model across fields. These changes have far-reaching consequences for the web regarding the monopolization, centralization, and exploitation of data resources.

One such project, Schema.org, started in 2011 and is the result of a partnership between Google, Microsoft, Yahoo, and Yandex—organizations that are traditionally commercial competitors but that decided to collaborate on a single structured data model for the web to benefit their search products (Guha et al., 2016). Today, millions of websites and applications use the Schema.org structured data model to assist with information search and retrieval. Users include news organizations verifying misinformation and fact-checking with structured data (Adair, 2020) and virtual assistant products such as Alexa and Google Assistant, which pull structured data from the web to answer queries (Kollar et al., 2018). Such practices often show the benefits of integrating web data across sites and applications using a single structured data model like Schema.org. Yet, the political and economic dimensions of the Schema.org partnership have been underexplored in the academic literature, and its ramifications for web users, organizations, and developers are not yet adequately attended to by scholars relative to its central role.

As infrastructures for facilitating information interoperability, structured data initiatives such as Schema.org are perhaps a less visible aspect of the web when compared to interfacial platforms like Facebook and Google. Yet, scholars have long emphasized the important and often invisible background work of information infrastructures (Bowker et al., 2009). Recent advancements in structured data modeling allow companies to leverage information infrastructures to crawl the machine-readable data on the web as if it were a single database of facts and assertions. This feature also helps these companies represent "knowledge" in their products, like the knowledge panels in search engine results and the maps and menus of service applications (Noy et al., 2019b, 2019c). Structured data thus increasingly provide an underlying semantics and context-control related to content for developers while also "intuitively" helping users find what they are looking for on apps and websites without relying on specific keywords in their searches.

Projects like Schema.org intend to avoid the convoluted intersection of multiple schemas, which can overburden web administrators, create confusion, and worsen the problem of harmonizing web information through a central structured data project. Yet, web developer critics of Schema.org have raised several problematic concerns relating to the political economy of platform companies' use of structured data (Andrews, 2020a, 2020b). This chapter addresses these critiques using network visualizations and archival research to provide critical analysis of Schema.org. It begins by discussing the origins of Schema.org in the early semantic web project (Berners-Lee & Fischetti, 1999). It reviews the literature on the political economy of web semantics and policy concerns related to standardized classificatory control mechanisms on the internet. I present data from Schema.org's release history along with a semantic network analysis and end the chapter by advocating for third-party regulators consisting of experts in social policy (and related areas) to moderate initiatives like Schema.org.

Semantic Platformization

Schema.org is, in some respects, a continuation of the platformization of the web. Inquiries into the social significance of digital tools like APIs have shown that such technologies facilitate platformization, which is said to entail "the extension of social media platforms into the rest of the web and their drive to make external web data 'platform ready'" (Helmond, 2015). Research into digital information infrastructures has developed adjacent to these platform-oriented approaches (Bowker et al., 2009; Edwards et al., 2009), with a subset focusing on online knowledge infrastructures (Edwards et al., 2013; Karasti et al., 2016) and their interoperability. More recently, there have been calls to combine these infrastructure and platform-based frameworks to examine information exchange mechanisms on the web through digital tools for knowledge sharing (Plantin et al., 2018a).

This chapter builds and extends work on these platform and infrastructure studies in what has been referred to as "knowledge as programmable object" (Plantin et al., 2018b) by focusing on recent advancements in structured data modeling across web platforms (Bates et al., 2016). As Bucher (2012a, 2012b) and Helmond (2015) show, data portability in the context of web platforms requires a certain level of semantic annotation. This semantic interoperability is among several defining features of the web, or what has been referred to by computer scientists as the "semantic web" (Antoniou et al., 2012; Szeredi et al., 2014). Since its inception as a global project reaching back to the beginnings of the web in the early 1990s, the semantic web has privileged the status of metadata for providing fine-grained levels of contextual expressivity needed for machine-readable web data. Web semantics are now commonplace in products like Google's Knowledge Graph (as discussed in the previous chapter), virtual assistants like Siri and Alexa that rely on Wikidata (the following two chapters discuss these), and other sources that engage markup in platformized versions of knowledge representation.

Schema.org

Schema.org is a modern outgrowth of the semantic web; its website states that the "data model used is [...] derived from RDF Schema," which was previously published by Berners-Lee's W3C (Brickley & Guha, 1999). Schema.org leadership has close ties to W3C. Members include Dan Brickley, who runs the daily operations for Schema.org and who is on the steering group as Google's representative (Brickley previously developed RDF and semantic web technology at W3C), and Guha (also now at Google), who initiated Schema.org. Guha previously co-edited the RDF Schema specification with Brickley. There is a direct line from the RDF Schema released in 1998 to the Schema.org of today (Lassila & Swick, 1999).

The histories of W3C and Schema.org are deeply intertwined. More recently, the Schema.org website states that "since April 2015, the W3C Schema.org Community Group is the main forum for collaboration" and that the current Chief Operating Officer of W3C Ralph Swick "helped establish the relations between Schema.org and the W3C." Though Schema.org has close ties to the W3C, it is not an official part of the W3C, nor is it considered one of their standards, indicating on their website that Schema.org is not "a standards body like the W3C."

Instead, Schema.org launched on June 2, 2011, as a joint project between Google, Microsoft, Yahoo, and Yandex to harmonize structured data on the web using logic and syntaxes like those provided by W3C. The site states that the project was "to make it easier for webmasters to provide us with data so that we may better direct users to their sites." Their frequently asked questions page explains some of the reasoning behind the partnership:

> Currently, there are many standards and schemas for marking up different types of information on web pages. As a result, it is difficult for webmasters to decide on the most relevant and supported markup standards to use. Creating a schema supported by all the major search engines makes it easier for webmasters to add markup, which makes it easier for search engines to create rich search features for users.[13]

Schema.org is a self-described "collaborative, community activity with a mission to create, maintain, and promote schemas for structured data on the Internet, on web pages, in email messages, and beyond." The website makes several other distinctions, including that the metadata "hierarchy presented on this site is not intended to be a 'global ontology' of the world [...] it is still the case that schema.org is not intended as a universal ontology." The site also claims that "applications from Google, Microsoft, Pinterest, Yandex, and others already use these vocabularies to power rich, extensible experiences." Schema.org is used across the web in the news domain by *The New York Times*, *The Guardian*, and the BBC; in movies by the Internet Movie Database (IMDb) and Rotten Tomatoes; and in places like WordPress, Yelp, LinkedIn, Alibaba, CVS, Soundcloud, and others.

Most of the studies mentioned previously in this book discuss the semantic web before the rise of Schema.org, focusing on historical and philosophical conceptions of the semantic web, notable standards bodies like the W3C, or public and institutional use of semantic web technologies. Few studies (Patel-Schneider, 2014; McCarthy, 2017) have attempted to examine Schema.org from critical, economic, or sociological perspectives, and those that do have not commented on the political economy of Schema.org as an organization and technology, nor have they provided any substantial empirical evidence of Schema.org's powerful positioning in the contemporary web. For details about Schema.org adoption and use, see the Web Data Commons' Schema.org Table Corpus, which shows that common schema vocabulary terms adopted across the web are entities such as "Product," "Person," "LocalBusiness," "CreativeWork," "Event," and "Place."

Schema.org presents itself as a community collaboration between non-profits, standards organizations, and corporate partners in the service of web administrators and users who will benefit from the structured data. Yet, it is curious that as a seemingly general use structured data model, Schema.org distances itself from the label of global or universal ontology. As web developer critics have noted (Andrews, 2020a, 2020b), there are open questions regarding the political economy of Schema.org concerning its structure, governance, and use in relation to Google and its monopolization of web data. Further institutional research should attempt to move beyond the manufactured appearance of Schema.org's self-presentation, which suggests it is a general-purpose schema yet not a global ontology, and a community collaboration but not a W3C or Google property.

Methods

I was interested in what types of vocabulary terms the Schema.org ontology included in its development history, and to investigate any significant areas of focus or other sociopolitical issues discernible from the metadata (such as whether or not there is any focus on social or free services). I want to mention here that I believe all technological systems are biased somehow. Thus, I am not seeking to "fix" a problem that researchers could ever resolve. Instead, I merely investigate what kinds of topics seem to have priority (possibly to the exclusion of others). Following Feinberg (2017) on the reading of databases, the purpose here is to conduct a hermeneutic process of reading Schema.org to see what its thrust is. As Feinberg states, reading a database "involves understanding the relationship between database structure and database content as an interpretation of the world."

I scraped the documented release history of the Schema. org updates from the Schema.org releases website and manually created a summary of the last ten releases' vocabulary additions. I ran the complete release history through Wordlist Maker to extract unique terms from the corpus, then removed non-schema-related words to isolate all schema terms in the release history, allowing me to see which terms it contains. I wanted to visualize Schema.org's ontology in a semantic network and for this I downloaded two comma-separated value (CSV) files (Types and Properties) containing the Schema.org ontology from the Schema.org developers page (schema.org/docs/developers .html) and processed it using Gephi (Bastian et al., 2009). Using Gephi's interaction techniques, I explored the Schema.org ontology and customized the visualization by expanding the hierarchy to display the nodes (representing vocabulary terms) and edges (representing subTypeOf relationships). After importing the CSV material to Gephi, the ForceAtlas2 layout algorithm was employed (Jacomy et al., 2014). The nodes were resized according to their degree ranking (min. 100 to max. 1,500).

Analysis and Findings

As of this writing, the Schema.org release history contains 13 major updates and 52 total updates, including minor updates ranging from release 0.91 (04/21/12) to release 13.0 (07/07/21). A sample summary of the kinds of terms included in the last ten releases is presented in table 3.1. The updates in these previous releases included metadata in biology and basic life science concepts, fact-checking and misinformation, floorplans and layout images, and school districts. There is no consistent logic concerning the release order or kinds of terms. Indeed, possible community extensions to Schema.org vocabulary are proposed and temporarily hosted on a pending ad hoc basis before they are incorporated into the Schema. org core. Such extensions include automotive, health and life sciences, and bibliographic fields. Schema.org's vocabulary currently consists of 792 Types, 1,447 Properties, 15 Datatypes, 83 Enumerations, and 445 Enumeration members.

In the Schema.org release history, 970 unique schema terms were discernible, relating to entities beyond the

Table 3.1: Summary of last 10 Schema.org updates as of 08/23/21

Recent Releases	Topics Added (excerpts)
13.0. 2021-07-07	• Biology and basic life science concepts, biochemistry, molecular entities, and chemicals. • Merchant return policies relating to return shipping, damaged products, labels, and policies. • Job applications and postings. • Fact-checking and misinformation labelling, including reviews of media and claims. • Casual opinion claims unrelated to news or factual records. • Positive and negative reviews. • Countries of processing and assembly.
12.0. 2021-03-08	• Ineligible regions. • Durations of media episodes. • Structured sizes and measurement. • Backorders and item availability. • Health aspects relating to vaccines, health access, allergies, safety, pregnancy. • Occupational experience and requirements.
11.0. 2020-11-30	• Offline and online events. • Animated stories. • Price types, invoices, down payments, cleaning fees, billing start and end dates. • Seeking and actions related to video content. • Math actions and solutions. • Learning and educational resources. • Copyright and credit notices.
10.0. 2020-09-07	• Educational questions, learning resources, and courses. • Floorplans and layout images. • Energy efficiency, consumption.
9.0. 2020-07-21	• Learning resources, creative works, and quizzes. • Product groups and variations. • Boat reservations and boat trips.
8.0. 2020-05-01	• Non-profit status, organizations, and types. • Delivery times, shipping destinations, rates, and details. • Citizenship, legal, and visa requirements for job postings.
7.04. 2020-04-16	• Hackathon types. • Start and end times for schedules.
7.03. 2020-04-02	• Hospital reporting.
7.02. 2020-03-31	• Special announcements and locations.
7.01. 2020-03-22	• School districts.

Source: Created by the author

core vocabulary. These terms were either added at some point or discussed for inclusion. They range across various fields, and some domain areas seem to count out of necessity based on current world events. Interesting domains are related to identifying actions, conducting content moderation, organizing broadcasting and educational activities, labeling energy consumption, identifying geography, describing "has" and "how" relationships for instructions, and identifying media artifacts. For example, designating actions on the web are described, such as acquiring license pages and applications, providing feedback policies, or giving opinions. Web administrators can use these to surface such actions in search results. Fact-checking and misinformation labeling are available through "review of claim" and "review of media" terms which news organizations can use to mark up their news stories and surface warnings in news feeds. Educational programs, credentials, occupations, events, and requirements terms are included for school facilitators to boost these data points in their profiles for potential students searching for information. The words range from relatively simple recipe ingredients to more complex terms relating to biochemical entities and biopolymer sequences.

These terms range from simple entities and relationships that "regular" everyday web users might be interested in finding in knowledge panels—examples include locating information about employment or education—to much more complex instances where specialists would likely be the beneficiaries when attempting to mark up and share web data. The range of complexity represented in the release history's unique terms indicates Schema.org's coverage and possible application areas, spanning several domains and industries.

While the unique terms in the release history point to areas that have recently been under development, Schema.org's current core vocabulary shows the earliest and seemingly most important "high-level" domains for the project. For example, Brickley (2019) presents the high-level items in the Schema.org hierarchy and displays them as a sunburst which includes top-level domains for vocabulary items relating to the categories of "Person," "Organization," "Place," "CreativeWork," "Intangible," "Action," "MedicalEntity," and "Event." The categories illustrate the datafication of life within several areas, from tech industries to creative work. These top-level domains are relatively abstract and less specific than the lower-level vocabulary items, clearly indicating that from the beginning, Schema.org was to organize its structured data across a wide variety of domains. Ribes et al. (2019) describe the logic of domains in computing and their relationship to meaning-making processes in machines and artificial intelligence.

My semantic network visualization of the Schema.org hierarchy is presented in figure 3.1; the nodes represent the top-level domains indicated in Brickley (2019) with a higher in-degree centrality (the number of ties directed to

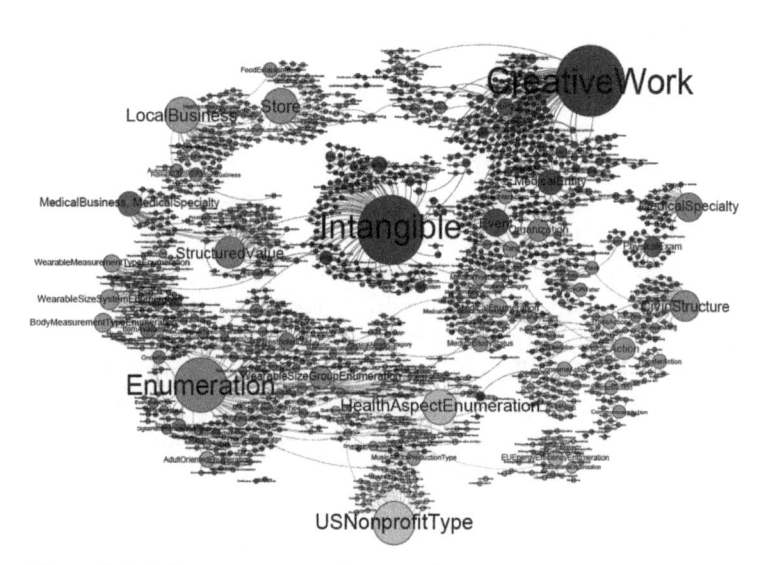

Figure 3.1: Schema.org semantic network

Source: Created by the author

a node). The figure shows several interesting features of the Schema.org core hierarchy, including which hierarchy terms are subclasses of higher-level domain terms. The visualization provides a more helpful way to examine the Schema.org complete hierarchy than merely scrolling through long lists of hierarchy terms. The semantic network contains 1,387 nodes and 1,344 edges in a directed graph. The network's modularity is 0.925, showing that the network is highly modular in nature with a number of communities at 73 and an average degree of 0.969.

For example, the "CreativeWork" category in the network is the third most connected node and includes media texts, production, and consumption entities. Here, creative works are understood as units or types of labor, illustrating tech companies' role in shaping normative cultural production and consumption standards in recent decades (Napoli & Caplan, 2017). Similarly, the "Place" categorization privileges locations related to culture, tourism, and commerce (i.e., where people are likely to spend money and leisure time). These essentially public locations are often involved in vacation and leisure contexts (e.g., "TouristAttraction," "LandmarksOrHistoricalBuildings," "CivicStructure"). Likewise, the "Event" item focuses on cultural events and texts (e.g., "ComedyEvent," "Festival," "ScreeningEvent," "ExhibitionEvent"). The "Intangible" category hierarchizes purchasing behaviors and commodities, a common theme among second-level entities.

Moreover, some items appear less tangible than others (i.e., the difference between making a reservation, purchasing a ticket, or enumeration). This category includes sub-items such as "Brand," "MerchantReturnPolicy," and "MediaSubscription." What is notable here is not necessarily how well these items fit within the assigned category but the extent to which each class defines purchasing behaviors, cultural commodities, and creative labor. The privileging of creative work and focus on cultural labor made possible through the services provided by platform companies illustrates the complex webs of meaning-making within these spheres and the role that Schema.org plays in legitimizing and making those meanings accessible to the people who search them frequently. Several other interesting entities appear in the hierarchy, including terms related to the COVID-19 pandemic and online fact-checking and misinformation.

Fact-Checks and Misinformation

Schema.org appears to be releasing terms to combat conspiracy theories and misinformation on the internet. One word, "ClaimReview," enables developers to mark up news stories with fact-checks to appear as such in search results. Google announced the display of this feature on October 13, 2016. The use of this tool grew in connection to the fake news debates surrounding the 2016 US presidential election (Bing introduced support for fact-checks using ClaimReview on September 14, 2017). ClaimReview positions Schema.org and Google as critical arbiters of what is credible, leveraging the perception of their widespread legitimacy as a source of information.

Alexios Mantzarlis, News and Information Credibility Lead at Google News Lab, writes that "fact-checking initiatives around the world mark up their work with ClaimReview, which allows fact-checkers to signal—and anyone online to automatically detect—that a webpage contains a fact check" (Mantzarlis, 2019). Google's Fact Check Explorer is a search feature to discover fact-checks, including those that use the ClaimReview markup. Academic researchers are also interested in ClaimReview and are involved in spreading literacy about the feature. The Duke Reporters' Lab runs the ClaimReview Project initiative that shares information about the fact-check function (Lim, 2019). There is also Full Fact, a registered charity that consists of "a team of independent fact checkers and campaigners who find, expose and counter the harm." Facebook and Google fund Full Fact; the charity works for these companies, including Facebook's Third-Party Fact Checking Program and Google's work on COVID-19 fact-checking.

A recent guest blog post from Schema.org about ClaimReview discusses the link to fact-checking (Dudfield & Dodds, 2021). The post is titled "Enriching ClaimReview for fact checkers" and written by Andrew Dudfield (Head of Automated Fact Checking at Full Fact) and Leigh Dodds (an open data expert). The post states that ClaimReview is one of the "hidden jewels" of the schema hierarchy. The authors also note that at Full Fact they have been "exploring ways to revise and extend the claim review metadata to provide more detail that might enable further reuse and labelling of content, and further insights into the fact checking process." These areas include consolidating the recommendations and examples for implementing the feature Google and Bing have included in their structured data markup documentation pages. Others describe expanding ClaimReview to include further term identifiers and linking, enriching the markup to include claims, including information about errors and corrections, and citing evidence.

COVID-19 and Data Commons

Schema.org's vocabulary about COVID-19 is another example of a growth topic area thanks to current world events. In the first two months of the pandemic, Schema.org fast-tracked the approval of terms in the schema hierarchy to assist with information search and retrieval related to the pandemic. The first such release occurred with version 7.0 on March 17, 2020 and included the fast-track release of terms such as "CovidTestingFacility," "SpecialAnnouncement," and "eventAttendanceMode." Material marked up with these terms can appear on

Google's Fact Check page for "Coronavirus," in Google and Bing knowledge panels, and is available for retrieval by apps and platforms. These schema features populate some of the rich search results that users can see, allowing them to look up information and possibly take actions concerning COVID-19. Schema.org is also helping a National Science Foundation-funded study for a semantic integration platform to fight COVID-19 (Zverina, 2020).

Another initiative tied to Schema.org relevant for COVID-19 is Data Commons, "an open knowledge database of statistical data started in collaboration with the U.S. Census, Bureau of Labor Statistics, World Bank, and many others" (Raghavan, 2020). This project assists with finding statistics and presenting them in the knowledge panels when searchers look for something like "Covid-19 cases in Philadelphia." Its website is "an open knowledge repository that combines data from public datasets using mapped common entities. It includes tools to easily explore and analyze data across different datasets without data cleaning or joining." Schema.org is one way these data can map to these familiar entities in emissions, health, water, energy, education, employment, income, and other areas. Specifically, the website states that "DataCommons. org builds upon on the vocabularies defined by Schema. org." Google officially announced that it was making Data Commons available directly in Google Search and knowledge panels as a new layer of their Knowledge Graph as of 2020. Since Google announced Dataset Search in 2020, it has indexed almost 25 million datasets; it is "a dataset-discovery tool that provides search capabilities over potentially all datasets published on the Web" and draws heavily on Schema.org (Noy et al., 2019a).

A Global Ontology for Whom?

There are many apparent benefits to Schema.org in terms of producing critical information for an international population during times of global crisis and political upheaval. Yet, its utility in surfacing relevant information in things like knowledge panels and virtual assistants also keeps people glued to those results rather than searching other sources. Companies like Google and Microsoft effectively become this semantic middle layer where information extracted from web pages marked up with Schema. org data is available in rich results. This process increases the foothold of large companies concerning the information that they produce in results, and it can diminish the traffic to those primary sources.

For example, knowledge panels partially populated by Schema.org markup contain information about items like biographical details and facts, which are a significant part of internet infrastructure for users today. Most notably, "62 percent of mobile searches in June 2019 were no-click" and "people ages 13 to 21" are "twice as likely" as people over 50 "to consider their search complete" once they've seen a "knowledge panel" (Kelley, 2019). Semantics provided by Schema.org will continue to play a role as users seek information from virtual assistants and knowledge panels, partly because they work, people use them, and many are not aware of the costs to the primary sources when search engines take data from them. Cases such as COVID-19 show apparent benefits to this type of information extraction, but there are many more "mundane" cases where a smaller publisher, who creates niche content or content they don't make a lot of money on, loses out.

By engineering software that processes structured data that provide descriptions of the world, companies like Google and Microsoft have designed technological infrastructure that privileges specific conceptualizations of work, labor, news, and life while limiting or ignoring alternatives. Schema.org acts as a regulator and gatekeeper through its ability to surface information in retrieval, potentially restricting access to information not defined or included in the markup or perhaps where errors have occurred. The job of social scientists and other researchers is now to locate examples of these limitations. For instance, researchers can begin surfacing semantic errors in information retrieval on products like Google's knowledge panels and Alexa's answers which rely partly on Schema.org. These semantic infrastructures assert what is possible, regular, and appropriate while consolidating information to benefit companies and corporations. The Schema.org partnership represents a critical juncture where tech companies have evolved programmable knowledge to govern how the web understands concepts such as labor, communication, cultural commodities, and media products. In doing so, platform companies have created hierarchies of searchable concepts while underscoring these processes with their marketing and cultural logic (Jenkins, 2004; van Dijck & Poell, 2013; Klinger & Svensson, 2014). Further social scientific research into structured data will make the organizational role of platform companies more transparent.

Since the beginning of the Schema.org ontology, the terms included span many domains. Schema.org is a global ontology, not a domain-specific one, contrary to its stated terms. The top-level domains seem reserved for abstract entities under which there is more specific domain information. Schema.org is a catch-22 for web developers in that they are encouraged to use the product to increase the visibility of their content while at the same time subject to how search engines operationalize Schema.org. Knowledge panels that present structured data keep traffic on their search products, illustrative of companies' attempts to monopolize information. Schema.org shapes expectations about what semantic technologies are suitable for in these ways. The point of defining standard vocabularies and creating structured data that use those vocabularies becomes focused on better integration with Google (search engine optimization). This process might exclude alternatives to the status quo of web crawling and algorithmic search as indispensable mediators between autonomous groups wanting to share information.

I spoke to information organization specialist Ryan Shaw (Shaw is an Associate Professor at the University of North Carolina at Chapel Hill's School of Information and Library Science). According to Shaw, one benefit of Schema.org is that "it has successfully cultivated a community process for maintaining and growing its vocabulary" (R. Shaw, pers. comm., April 1, 2022). Yet, as Shaw relayed to me, it has tended to "perpetuate the idea that there should be just one such community because it is inefficient or overly complex to have too many choices." In Shaw's view, we should be encouraging "the development of dozens of Schema.org-like projects, rather than assuming that once the problem of representing (e.g., medical information) has been 'solved,' then no one else need do it." According to Shaw, questions of data representation are not solvable. Instead, we would "all benefit from multiple different yet partially overlapping approaches to them"—something Shaw sees Schema.org as discouraging. Instead, he envisions a world where semantic media production becomes something not only for companies like Google and the tech elite but as something in which "groups of all sizes and purposes can engage." The role of such professionals "would be akin to public accountants who could audit the semantic media pipelines and warrant that the infoboxes mean what the substantive authors claim they do."

Schema Governance

As a final note, I acknowledge the critical role that a potential content moderating committee may serve in overseeing standard schema constructions on the internet in the public interest. In the same way that content moderation committees have been highlighted recently in social media (Gillespie, 2018; Roberts, 2019), I envision regulatory committees of specialists who may draw on their expertise in politics, journalism, media and communication, and social services. Such researchers may provide an essential social role in the construction of schema standards which can benefit from focusing on the social good and social services. Thus, the logic of such schemas may shift from serving not mainly areas of commercialization and social interest like public emergencies but further persisting structural inequalities around identity and access to information and resources for underserved communities.

Another issue that is central to the political economy of Schema.org is the nature of its schema governance. Most terms in Schema.org are for financially oriented topics relating to logistics, purchasing, traveling, etc. Less focus is on areas that might benefit socioeconomically under-privileged groups. For example, as far as I can tell, there is, as of this writing, no clear information relating to pro bono legal or immigration services (though there are terms for general legal services). There is no information on shelters for humans (rather than pets). There are no food drive terms (instead of fast food), no data on retirement homes (rather than hotels), etc. A more significant subclass is for stores (including outlets, liquor, and pawn) rather than stores providing free goods. The hierarchy aims at those who are already privileged.

Part of the reason for this is, I suspect, an outcome of Schema.org's governance, which mainly includes personnel who work for or affiliate with Google. According to the website, it is unclear if Microsoft, Yahoo, and Yandex still have personnel affiliated with the project. Considering this, Schema.org can expand its governance structure by including individuals who are not associated with large platform companies and who have expertise in areas such as social services. Such researchers would bring a critical eye to the kinds of topics included and help shift the focus away from commercial entities toward more just outcomes related to structured data on the web. Doing so would not be an unprecedented step, as platform companies have recently added committees that focus on content moderation issues. Schema governance should include non-researchers in the community and non-specialists who engage in search tasks in different contexts throughout the day. More diverse people may be included in schema governance in these ways, rather than only those who work at for-profit platforms. The utility is essential, but there must also be work on those schema areas that are less profitable and help underserved peoples.

Second, we should encourage Schema.org's governance to focus on expanding the languages in Schema.org. As it stands, Schema.org is in English, and this means that non-English speakers may be unable to participate in structured data practices. Schema.org should offer translations of the hierarchy so that developers can understand the differences in translation from one entity to the next. Translations should accompany the project if it aspires to be an open, community project. I make these recommendations not to imply that these issues can be resolved fully or let large platform companies off the hook once they attend to the problems. Instead, I think suggestions like these can be helpful to envision alternative and more radical projects and to critique the (often unjustified) claims of "neutrality" and "openness" that such companies and organizations often make.

Overall, Schema.org could be more transparent and forthcoming with its governance structure and describe who benefits from its structured data. If Google wishes to avoid accusations of monopolistic practices and antitrust suits, it must rethink how it uses Schema.org in its products. As I mentioned, Schema.org is a catch-22 for developers who must use the schema for their content to appear in search results or risk becoming less visible. Yet, the very nature of schema means that rich search results display site content. The consequences include fewer people visiting sites once they get the information they need directly from another large search company.

Schema.org and Google are closely linked. By engineering software that analyzes structured data, Google has designed infrastructures that privilege a consumerist approach to representation on the web while limiting or ignoring alternatives. Schema.org represents a critical juncture where tech companies have evolved to govern the way entities are defined, understood, and accessed on the web through semantic search. Further social scientific research into structured data will make the organizational role of platform companies more transparent in the areas of knowledge representation on the web. I view the task of researchers moving forward as locating examples of these limitations in critical search engine studies. For example, researchers may surface semantic errors in information retrieval on products like knowledge panels and virtual assistant answers which rely on the markup that Schema. org provides or may conduct studies to see what content areas they omit.

4

The Wiki Wrangler

Many of us know about Wikipedia, but most casual internet users likely have not heard of Wikidata (the common source knowledge base containing facts from Wikipedia). Wikipedia is, of course, the community-sourced online encyclopedia that people use when they want to look something up casually. Several scholarly books have documented the rise, organization, nature, and social implications of Wikipedia, each addressing different aspects of the project. Ayers et al. (2008) and Lih (2009) provide an account of Wikipedia, which itself started in 2001. McDowell and Vetter's more recent *Wikipedia and the representation of reality* (2021) offers another overview. Tkacz's *Wikipedia and the politics of openness* (2014) provides a sustained political critique of the project, highlighting contested terrain and battles fought over editing, policy decisions, and accessibility, while Bruckman's *Should you believe Wikipedia?* (2022) takes up issues of identity, community, and the construction of knowledge.

Wikipedia has well-documented sociocultural biases, including "Wikipedia's policies, practices, content, and participation" (Koerner, 2020). For example, Tripodi (2021) provides evidence of Wikipedia's gender bias through an ethnography of Wikipedia "edit-a-thons" and examining the metadata of Wikipedia articles listed for deletion. The research found that many pieces are about men and that editors recommend articles about women for deletion as being not notable enough. Another project by Sun and Peng (2021) involved an event-centric study of the Wikipedia corpus using machine learning. The authors found gender bias in the events recorded and described on Wikipedia; women's personal lives are often intermingled with their professional careers in the descriptions, whereas this occurs less frequently for the men. These results should not be surprising; Matei and Britt (2017) found that most of Wikipedia (77%) is written by only 1% of its contributors. In earlier research, Matei and Dobrescu (2011) found ambiguity in Wikipedia's neutrality policy, enabling personal biases to reflect how users take up these policies. "A taxonomy of knowledge gaps for Wikimedia projects" (Redi et al., 2020) outlines more of these problems.

Still, every major search engine, digital assistant, and countless other apps and services use Wikipedia. The company recently founded Wikipedia Enterprise, which sells Wikipedia content to large internet companies (Cohen, 2021). And it plays a central role in populating the knowledge panels that we discussed in the introduction and chapter 2. For better or worse, Wikipedia will continue to supply information to media companies, and those media companies will continue to present this information in their products. But relatively newer data technologies such as Wikidata will introduce new affordances and problems into this landscape.

Wikidata

One element of Wikipedia that is somewhat less popularly known, at least among those not in information science circles, is Wikidata, a collaborative knowledge base. Schema.org (discussed in the previous chapter) is an ontology codified into metadata that can "tag" web data to make it ingestible for a knowledge graph. Wikidata, on the other hand, resembles a knowledge base like the examples we discussed in chapter 2. However, as of late, some personnel affiliated with the project prefer not to see it as a knowledge base of facts, for reasons that will become clear in a moment. This hesitancy is similar to how, as discussed in the previous chapter, Schema.org prefers not to see itself as a "global ontology" to avoid the appearance that it has an influential position concerning naming and identifying things on the internet. Wikidata likewise has an ontology of its centralized base of knowledge. Wikidata is somewhat like Freebase; it is an extensive database of facts and assertions. Every entity in Wikidata is a fact that connects to other facts, and virtual assistants and search engines treat entries in Wikidata as such. While Freebase, as we already covered in chapter 2, was obtained by Google, Wikidata is likewise heavily used by Google as an open-source technology.

Wikidata was launched in 2012 as a "free, collaborative, multilingual, secondary database, collecting structured data to provide support for Wikipedia" (Vrandečić, 2020). Vrandečić and Krötzsch (2014) introduce Wikidata, calling it a "free collaborative knowledgebase." The abstract reads, in sum: "This collaboratively edited knowledgebase provides a common source of data for Wikipedia, and everyone else." The Wikidata website currently describes the project as "the free knowledge base with 96,017,063 data items that anyone can edit." The referenced knowledge base contains simple facts and statements encoded using triples. Currently, the project has over 13 billion triples derived from over 96 million Wikidata entities. The service receives requests for access (apps and people that want to use the knowledge base) in the range of tens of millions of hits each day. Wikidata can be searched and queried using the W3C-created SPARQL Protocol and RDF Query Language. It can also be visualized and connected to apps via the Wikidata Query Service and APIs.

Several academic projects use Wikidata, from constructing knowledge graphs for COVID-19 information (Turki et al., 2022), to being used by the Smithsonian (Pablo, 2020), to the Linked People project, which extracts data from Wikidata to create knowledge graphs about the connections between families and characters in film and television. A real-world equivalent is the EntiTree project, which helps visualize Wikidata items about people, organizations, and events in graph form. Other researchers have attempted to use knowledge bases such as Wikidata as a source of factual knowledge to model language models in machine learning (Safavi & Koutra, 2021).

Let's look at a relatively benign example of how to use Wikidata. In figure 4.1, the Kardashian extended family

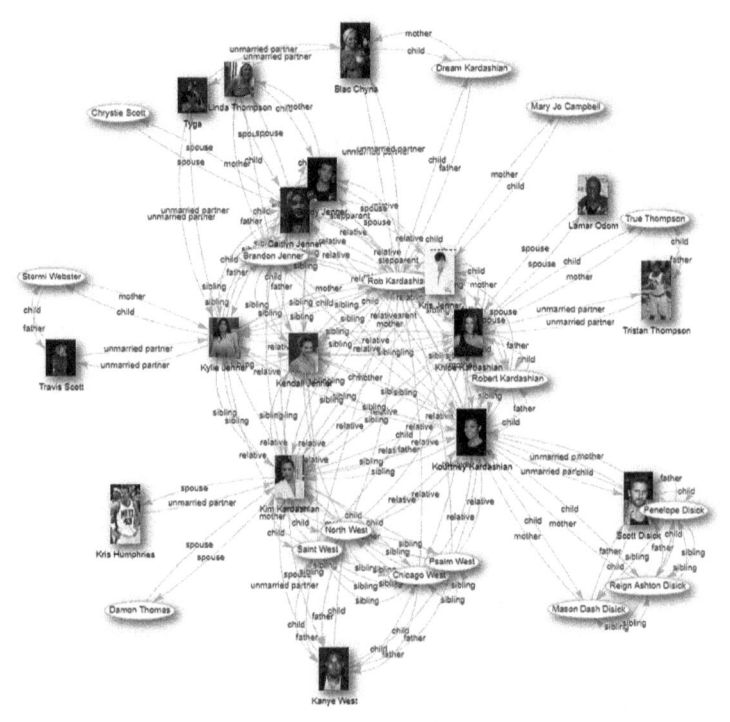

Figure 4.1: Kardashian family as extracted from Wikidata

Source: Created by the author

and their relationships are represented in a graph visualization using queried data from Wikidata. These data result from my search of the Wikidata Query Service using SPARQL Protocol. The graph displays Kardashian family members. Each family member is a node in the network, and there is information concerning their relationships in the in-between links. These directed edges are predicates that indicate the familial relationship, such as "daughter," "mother," etc. One can produce a similar visualization about any group of interlinked or related people, places, and things in Wikidata, so long as the information is in the database.

It is straightforward to visualize relationships between notable people. I was successful in conducting similar searches for lists of people and groups designated as terrorists by the United States. One can imagine searching for the networks and families of notable individuals who are currently experiencing crises, such as notable victims of crimes, prisoners, or politicians. There may be politically sensitive scenarios where the ability to collect these social networks on Wikidata may negatively affect individuals captured in the graph.

Wikidata contains structured information in the form of entities described as subjects, predicates, and objects, just like semantic triples, except the subject in a Wikidata entity is called an "item," the predicate is called a "property," and the object is called the "value." The subjects and items are things, the predicates and properties are relationships, and the objects and values are other things. So, for something like the example above, one can use semantic media products that query Wikidata statements about the Kardashian family members beyond simply their familial relationships. Examples include statements concerning their country of citizenship, where they were born, their occupation, where they went to school, their city of residence, what their ethnic group is, or to which political party they belong. These details represent the kind of information stored as structured data in each of the family members' Wikidata pages. While some of this information is also in the everyday natural language of Wikipedia pages, the Wikidata pages that contain this structured data allow for complex semantic querying.

There are many complex questions that services like Wikidata can answer (or other semantic media technologies, for that matter). Wikidata allows automated machines like search engines and digital assistants' APIs to look up semantically rich questions. Examples include "Names of 100 cities with a population larger than 1,000,000 in the native languages of their countries," "Current U.S. members of the Senate with district, party and date they assumed office," and "People who lived in the same period as another person." These are all real query examples taken from the Wikidata SPARQL query examples page—users may visit the page and try running these queries, which is relatively easy. Each subject and object must have its page on Wikidata; in this respect, Wikidata is very brittle in that the knowledge it contains must conform to its data model. If you want to quickly see the Wikidata on an average Wikipedia page, just hit Alt + Shift + G. It will flip from the regular Wikipedia page to the Wikidata page. Figure 4.2 shows the various components of a typical Wikidata entry.

Each entity in Wikidata is assigned a "Q" number; for example, in figure 4.2, the "Q" identifier number (Q42) is for identifying the entity "Douglas Adams" (the famous author of *The Hitchhiker's Guide to the Galaxy*). There are also the relevant information terms around that entity which include the label ("Douglas Adams"), description ("English writer and humorist"), property ("educated at"), value ("St John's College"), qualifiers ("academic major"), and other information. By way of another, more abstract example, the Wikidata object for "everyday life" is "Q1129653" and is described as "routine processes in humans daily and weekly cycle," and its Freebase ID is "/m/07wkk6." In Wikidata, it is a subclass of "human condition," an instance of a "habit," part of a "personal

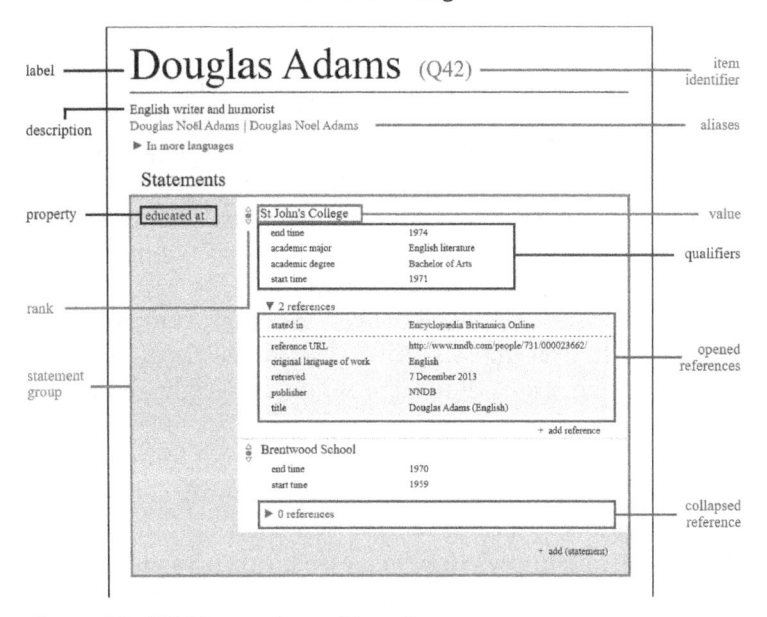

Figure 4.2: Wikidata entity and its values

life," has the quality of being "diurnal," and is said to be the same as a "daily routine." This description is a non-insignificant amount of data about something like the concept "everyday life" for a knowledge base to grasp. Now replicate this type of understanding with millions and billions of examples, and you have a rough idea of the power of Wikidata for naming things and relationships and articulating facts about them.

In these ways, Wikidata atomizes the unstructured language contained within Wikipedia articles and across the whole knowledge base into discrete bits of semantic triples. It is as though Wikidata has distilled the "bare" facts from the information contained in Wikipedia in a highly structured way. Gone are the narratives, rich background histories, stories from academic sources and news articles, detailed descriptions of people's deaths, childhood upbringings, and more. What is left is a database of facts, which themselves are interrelated, and which are queryable, allowing individuals to obtain quick answers, bite-sized knowledge, and limited data related to a specific question. Wikidata is the underlying logical and informational infrastructure that undergirds the wordier and more descriptive Wikipedia. It contains packaged facts that are ready to go, making sense, given Wikipedia's emphasis on transparency and sharing information.

Indeed, one of Wikidata's guiding principles is openness. It uses the Creative Commons Zero, or CC0 license, which states that there is "no copyright reserved" even for commercial purposes. Other principles include sustainability (it focuses on long-term and foundational resources rather than growth), co-creation (it depends on editors), utility (a desire to have Wikidata used outside of Wikidata), and knowledge equity (focusing on a plurality of knowledge). There are conferences and events dedicated to the project and maintaining these principles. WikidataCon is a yearly event featuring research and talks about Wikidata and the community. It is perhaps unsurprising that WikidataCon 2021 was sponsored by, among others, Google, Apple, Amazon, and Wolfram. With its licensing and sponsors, the knowledge contained in Wikidata is prime for the taking in semantic media products.

Upper Ontology

An ontology organizes information about Wikidata entities like those for the Kardashian family discussed above. In a sense, this ontology "grounds" or contains all of the statements and facts expressed through Wikidata. As discussed in chapter 1, computational ontologies are formalized metadata vocabularies for organizing data. Ontologies can be "domain-specific" (meaning they can be about a topic or field, containing specific terms related to that field). Or they can be "upper level" to provide logical rules for combining multiple domain-specific ontologies and sets of data. For example, as we saw in the previous chapter with the Schema.org case study, that particular web schema has an ontology with upper-level terms that then descend in a treelike structure of subclasses and superclasses to more specific domain terms. It is a reasonably market-focused ontology since its aim is, arguably, to provide better search engine optimization for companies like Google.

Like the schema discussed in chapter 3, Wikidata, as a knowledge base, also has an upper-level ontology that is used to organize the data. Also, like the schema example, Wikidata can be considered an upper-level ontology because it acts as a way to organize all domain-specific information. For example, the Blood Ontology (in the medical field) and the Financial Industry Business Ontology (in commerce) attempt to manage metadata categories for those topics and the entities in their domain. Sometimes these heterogeneous ontologies need to be interoperable if there is any attempt to combine the data they reference. This example is where upper-level ontologies like the one provided by Wikidata come in; these ontologies create highly abstract ways of categorizing entities and relations in the world (think back to our discussion on ontology in the first chapter) that are domain-independent. Only a handful of these upper ontologies found wide use, including Basic Formal Ontology (BFO), Descriptive Ontology for Linguistic and Cognitive Engineering (DOLCE), and Suggested Upper Merged Ontology (SUMO), among others. While these have been used in many areas to help make data interoperable across domains, large platform companies on the internet mainly use the Schema.org and Wikidata upper ontologies.[14]

Typically, these upper-level ontologies must be "small" because they contain abstract ways to categorize entities and relations. They are traditionally not supposed to have domain-specific terms but rather only the conceptual categories under which those terms can fall—things like abstract descriptions of entities, qualities, and relationships. So, upper-level ontologies are closer to philosophical ontology since they apply to all domains. For example, their top-level category will usually be called something like "entity" or "thing" which would then be divided into subareas.

Wikidata's Ontology

Wikidata has an upper-level ontology, but it also has a page indicating that it aspires or will attempt to reconcile other top-level ontologies (like BFO, DOLCE, etc.). The WikiProject Ontology page states that the Wikidata ontology "is mainly about reaching deep into the nature of being, becoming, existence, and reality, and applying those insights during Wikidata's maintenance tasks." The practical aims that it describes include: "to support a broad semantic interoperability between notable ontologies like DOLCE, BFO, SUMO, Lemon, RDA, etc.," "to build consensus around the main branches of our core concept tree and how they relate to each other," and "to gain a deep understanding about the meaning of our upper ontology and to transfer this knowledge to others in practical terms." It almost sounds like Wikidata's ontology is attempting to position itself at the very top of all upper ontologies as *the ultimate* ontology. Whether something like that is achievable is questionable since, as we have seen, it is difficult if not impossible for *everyone* to agree on an ontology, though one may argue that the "winner" of these upper-level ontology wars is simply the ontology that finds the widest usage. In this case, that winner might be Wikidata since Wikipedia is one of the largest collaborative initiatives on the web. Even so, the other upper-level ontologies that exist are not likely to disappear as some have become official international standards and new projects are likely to appear. Readers might be familiar with the humorous xkcd webcomic titled "How standards proliferate" (xkcd.com/927) where the first panel reads "Situation: There are 14 competing standards." In the next panel, one stick-figure person says to another "14?! Ridiculous! We need to develop one universal standard that covers everyone's use cases." The other stick-figure person enthusiastically replies with a "Yeah!" Then, on the last panel, the text reads: "Situation: There are 15 competing standards."

Methods

I wanted to investigate Wikidata's ontology, similar to the Schema.org example in chapter 3. While Wikidata's ontology is not immediately visible, there are ways to look at some of its contents. Like the Schema.org developer page, Wikidata contains pages documenting the ontology, and some of them provide information about querying the entities and relationships. I used the Wikidata Query Service and ran a SPARQL query looking for Wikidata's top-level ontology. The query example using SPARQL code is as follows:

```
SELECT ?item ?superclass WHERE {
  VALUES ?top { wd:Q35120 }
  {
    ?item wdt:P279 ?top .
    BIND( ?top AS ?superclass ) .
  } UNION {
    ?item wdt:P279 ?superclass .
    ?superclass wdt:P279 ?top .
  }
  } ORDER BY ( ?superclass != ?top ) DESC(
?superclass ) ASC( ?item )
```

Once the query returned results, I downloaded the ontology as a comma-separated values (CSV) file using the Wikidata Query Service export option. I then imported the CSV file and visualized the top-level ontology using Gephi software (Bastian et al., 2009) to see some of the top terms. I used the Yifan Hu and Label Adjust graph visualization algorithms (Hu, 2005) to represent the data and examine the nodes and edges. There are currently 626 items described on the WikiProject Ontology page, while my visualization had 643 nodes and 644 edges in a directed graph. I ran modularity statistics (Blondel et al., 2008) and adjusted color, size, and label features to increase node size, separate labels to make things more transparent, etc. These steps allowed me to better visualize the graph. I then exported the visualization from Gephi.

Results

Figure 4.3 shows the Wikidata top-level terms in the Wikidata ontology represented in Gephi. It shows their connectedness concerning in-degree centrality (recall, this is the number of ties directed to a node). For example, the nodes (entities) with the highest in-degree are Q15989253, which represents the term "Part," defined as a "separate element of a larger (divisible or indivisible) entity," and Q488383, which means "Object," described as "anything that exists and may be acted upon by a subject." Others include Q937228, which represents "Property," defined as a "predominant feature that characterizes a being, a thing, a phenomenon, etc. and which differentiates one being from another, one thing from another;" and Q35120, which represents "Entity," defined as "anything that can be considered, discussed, or observed." Many of the other top-level terms fall under these categories. It is not hard to see how this language resembles that of philosophical ontology discussed in some of the previous chapters. Wikidata's upper-level ontology has a modularity of 0.806 and has 17 communities, with an average degree of 1.002.

There are many interesting terms in Wikidata's top-level ontology list, which seems broader and messier than the one represented in Schema.org. Below are some of the interesting entities in the Wikidata ontology that I selected as examples. Many of these vocabulary terms

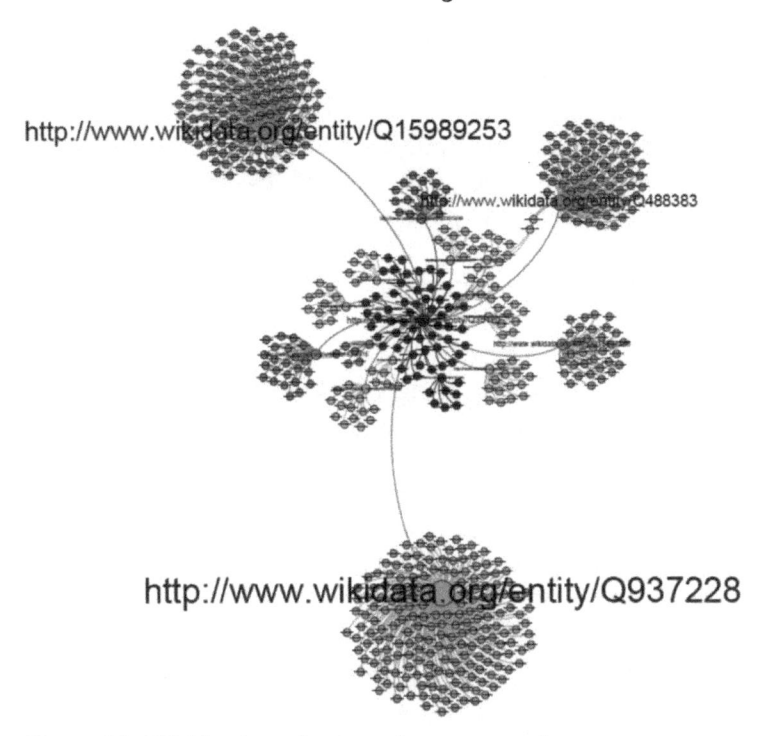

http://www.wikidata.org/entity/Q15989253

http://www.wikidata.org/entity/Q488383

http://www.wikidata.org/entity/Q937228

Figure 4.3: Wikidata's top-level ontology as a graph

Source: Created by the author

are ambiguous in nature, if not blatantly subjective or contested, and one can easily imagine disagreements that might occur concerning their definitions and applications:

- Meaning ("nature of meaning in the philosophy of language, semantics, metaphysics and metasemantics")
- Hypothetical entity ("entity whose existence is possible, but not proven")
- Being ("broad concept encompassing objective and subjective features of reality and existence")
- Urbanity ("characteristics, personality traits, and viewpoints associated with cities and urban areas")
- Pricelessness ("state or condition of being priceless; very high value")

- Greatness ("concept of a state of superiority affecting a person or object in a particular place or area")
- Acceptability ("characteristic of a thing being subject to acceptance for some purpose")
- Critically acclaimed ("acclaimed by critics; that has received generally good reviews from a number of critics")
- Mental property ("property of the mind")
- Disability ("impairments, activity limitations, and participation restrictions")
- Undead ("deceased being which behaves as if alive")
- Agent ("individual and identifiable entity capable of performing actions")
- Heritage ("property, custom, or other material, immaterial or natural object inherited from previous generations, and conserved for its importance for future generations")
- Bad ("item with negative value to the consumer")
- Banned object ("entity that has been censored by somebody")
- Extinct language ("language that no longer has any speakers")

Researchers have created modeling theories to assess the taxonomic hierarchies in Wikidata (Brasileiro et al., 2016). Understanding Wikidata's taxonomy and ontology are essential because they are involved in organizing and labeling the information that exists in Wikidata. Earlier in this chapter, we described how statements exist as Wikidata entities that have values attributed to them in the form of triples. The ontology and taxonomy organize these statements according to their rules and logic. There are interesting consequences regarding the "truth" and semantic meaning of facts expressed through Wikidata. Wikidata essentially acts as a modern-day philosopher that gets to define and describe what exists and the sense of things. Some of the terms listed above are fairly ambiguous; what makes something priceless, great, acceptable, a disability, a part of a heritage, banned, or bad? These are the vague areas with which Wikidata's ontology concerns itself.

Just the Facts

Wikidata has another not-so-obvious ambiguity problem. Wikidata states facts about the world, and not all these facts are attributable to sources. Figure 4.4 shows that most facts on Wikidata link to references, but there is still a sizeable portion (almost a quarter) that do not; Wikidata labels these as "unreferenced statements." Many statements are only "referenced to Wikipedia" and not any other source. Kolbe (2015) raises these concerns and criticizes Wikidata's unreferenced statements, which make up roughly half of the content on Wikidata.

A statement in Wikidata is, according to Wikidata's "Statements" page, "a concept, topic, or object" represented by an item with its page. The description continues by referencing W3C's semantic RDF data model and relates that a "statement (Resource Description Framework (Q54872) graph format: Subject-Predicate-Object) is how the information we know about an item—the data we have about it—gets recorded in Wikidata." So, RDF

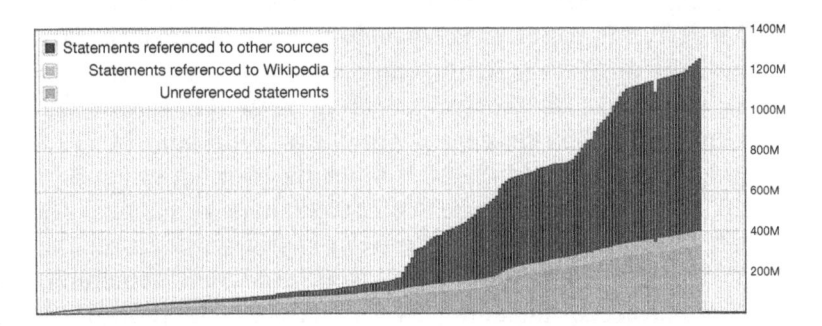

Figure 4.4: Wikidata statements and references as of Nov 30, 2021

Source: Wikidata Stats: wikidata-todo.toolforge.org/stats.php. Courtesy of Magnus Manske.

triples (subjects, predicates, objects) model information about entities in Wikidata. Many of these statements are unreferenced—Ford's book, *Writing the revolution: Wikipedia and the survival of facts in the digital age* (2022), examines these facts and Wikipedia. Other criticisms that Wikidata is open to include that third parties could use Wikidata on their apps and sites without providing proper attribution, even for the facts that have references. This lack of attribution is because the license for Wikidata is exceptionally minimal, thus not encouraging users to provide provenance information. When a fact is taken from Wikidata and used in something like a virtual assistant, there is no incentive for companies to attribute the data to a source; they can merely take the information and use it in their products. Another problem is that Wikidata is, like Wikipedia, vulnerable to hoaxes. The same types of mistakes, sociocultural biases, errors, and lies sometimes found on Wikipedia can also make their way to Wikidata.

Kolbe (2015) notes that the original €1.5 million in funding for Wikidata in 2012 came from Microsoft co-founder Paul Allen's Institute for Artificial Intelligence. A quarter came from Google and another quarter from Intel co-founder Gordon E. Moore and the Gordon and Betty Moore Foundation. Denny Vrandečić led the original developers and previously worked on the Semantic MediaWiki project, which sought to include semantic data in wiki pages. In 2013, Vrandečić also began work as an ontologist at Google, assisting with the Knowledge Graph while continuing in his role at Wikidata. In 2015 he joined the board of the Wikimedia Foundation, and in 2019 he became Google's Wikimedian in Residence. He left Google in 2020 and is currently still working for the Wikimedia Foundation on existing and new structured data projects, including Wikifunctions (collaboratively sourced computer functions).

Interestingly, contrary to some early definitions of Wikidata, as well as the facts above concerning Wikidata's lack of references and ability to verify some claims, Wikidata now has a "Verifiability" page which states:

> Wikidata is not a database that stores facts about the world, but a secondary knowledge base that collects and links to references to such knowledge. This means that Wikidata does not state what the population of Germany actually is; it simply provides the information on what the population of Germany is according to a specific source, such as The World Factbook (Q11191).

It is interesting to see Wikidata now describe itself as a "secondary database" and not a "database that stores facts about the world" as per the original research paper describing the project. The rhetorical move here is reminiscent of the one made by Schema.org when it claims that it is not a "global ontology." While it may be true that there are now a higher number of statements referenced in Wikidata than those not referenced, there is still a sizable amount of unreferenced content. The other criticisms listed by Kolbe remain, including that the data from Wikidata can be used by anyone, including the products of platform companies, without having to be referenced at all, making it appear as though, say, Alexa or Google Assistant was providing you with the information. Questions will always remain concerning the centralization of this knowledge as it funnels through significant media technology companies and how it is carved out, a process that could perpetuate sociocultural biases (as in the case with Wikipedia itself) or reduce verifiability.

Common Knowledge?

Some critics argue that Wikidata does not promote knowledge diversity. Vrandečić has stated that the idea that Wikidata, "from which any of the individual language Wikipedias can draw content from, will necessarily reduce this diversity, is false" (2020). Still, some argue that Wikidata omits and sidelines some types of knowledge and epistemologies. The edited collection *Wikipedia @ 20* (Reagle & Koerner, 2020) contains contributions from Wikidata leaders like Vrandečić and the projects' critics. Ford (2020) writes that Wikidata "has millions of statements that are either uncredited to a reliable source or attributed to the entire Wikipedia." Ford notes that this does not meet Wikipedia's requirements for verifiability in that it does not allow people to trace the provenance of facts and statements. She also describes how recently many major platform companies use Wikidata in media products such as digital assistants like Alexa and Siri. Following Kolbe (2015), Ford notes that without quality control, errors in Wikidata are found downstream in the platforms that use Wikidata to present facts and information to their users (we will look at these, including virtual assistants, in the final chapter).

In an illuminating conversation between Ford and Vrandečić (2020), Ford states that projects like Wikidata are "dominant" representations that can "affect people well beyond the wiki and around the world" in that it is "a global consensus view about people, places, events and things around the world." The likely effect that Wikidata will have is enormous, and a similar sentiment is in the popular press. *Wired* magazine recently noted that "as platforms like Google and Alexa work to provide instant answers to random questions, Wikidata will be one of the critical architectures that link the world's information together" (Cooke, 2021). In a *TechCrunch* article published around the release of Wikidata, the authors describe it as a "new effort to provide a database of knowledge that can be read and edited by humans and machines alike." Wikidata "will bring all the localized versions of Wikipedia on par with each other in terms of the basic facts they house," and will "enable users to ask different types of questions, like which of the world's ten largest cities have a female mayor?" (Pérez, 2012).

Wikidata aspired to be a global knowledge base of facts, adopting a large consensus view.

Ford has been a longtime critic of Wikidata. As mentioned in the introduction, Ford and Graham (2016a) identified issues around Wikidata concerning knowledge diversity and verifiability at an early stage. For example, they note how information about "Paris," across hundreds of language versions of Wikipedia and different media in those language versions, all now feed back into Wikidata. Wikidata links to data about "Paris" from "across Wikimedia projects (in addition to other sources of data from across the web) so that it becomes the central site for those wanting to reuse data." They noted that most Wikidata statements remained unsourced. Most discussions about sourcing occurred in English, not to mention a general lack of people who have experience working with structured data. Ford and Graham also note that corporations like Google profit from Wikidata while not providing provenance data. This process is complicated, they say, "for opponents of Wikidata and Google's semantic web activities to articulate exactly what the problem with this loss of provenance is and why it is so important to integrate provenance data when websites share information." Ultimately, lack of provenance in Wikidata and Google "leads to users losing their ability to effectively engage with the origins (and thus contexts and biases) of a statement" (Ford and Graham, 2016a).

Critical scholars and researchers are paying attention to Wikidata, it seems. Anasuya Sengupta is a Wikimedian (she joined the Wikimedia Foundation in 2012) and co-director (with Adele Vrana and Siko Bouterse) of the Whose Knowledge? project.[15] The project seeks to, among other things, interrogate biased knowledge representations on the internet and decolonize Wikidata by focusing on knowledge justice for structured data. Sengupta, who recently gave a keynote at WikidataCon 2021, asked the audience to focus on knowledge justice (what kinds of knowledge does Wikidata include and exclude?) rather than only on the technical aspects of knowledge representation (a more analytical and less humanistic problem). She called for a focus on how these data are framed and reframed in terms of communities that express their knowledge differently and on bringing marginalized groups into administrative and policy discussions about knowledge representation projects such as Wikidata. For example, Graham and Sengupta (2017) state, "We're all connected now, so why is the internet so white and western?" Projects like the above examine the cultural and racial biases of Google and Wikipedia, and studies have confirmed these biases. Poulter and Ahmed's (2021) "Representation of non-western cultural knowledge on Wikipedia: The case of the visual arts" states that researchers "found just under four times as many statements about Western artists as non-Western artists, and nine times as many statements about Western as non-Western masterpieces." Decolonizing projects like Wikipedia and Wikidata will happen through more critical research about these knowledge representation biases. This approach can be started by including more provenance data about non-Western entities and by expanding the editorship and leadership roles to include members of the Global South.

The Spread of Wikidata

There are apparent problems with Wikidata concerning how it sources its data, the degree to which it enables verifiability and provenance, and how it is creating a centralized place for common knowledge that can exclude localized and epistemic cultural understandings. Yet, it would be unfair not to mention some of the many academic projects that use Wikidata, including those in the digital humanities. For example, Kat Thornton and Kenneth Seals-Nutt's Science Stories project uses Wikidata to tell multimedia stories about scientists, including those from underrepresented groups. Wilson (2020) describes

Mbabel, which contributes to Wikipedia and "automatically generates article drafts based on information stored on the 'web semantic database,' Wikidata." Wikidata's Schema.org page describes collaborations between the projects, including using Wikidata as a joint base for Schema.org when identifying "sameAs" relationships (a schema vocabulary term for saying something "is the same as" something else). Curotto and Hogan (2020) "explore automated methods for locating references that support" Wikidata claims. Ilievski et al. (2020) have run experiments testing for relevant, common sense knowledge in Wikidata that is representable as maps. There is also the WikiGenomes project, a "freely open, editable, and centralized model organism database for the biological research community," powered by Wikidata. Another project, the Witches digital humanities project, seeks to "geographically locate the residence location" of "accused witches" and map them out using Wikidata. There are many other examples of Wikidata's use in academic research beyond the technical realm of strict information science.

Unsurprisingly, some see Wikidata as having inherent liberatory and social justice qualities. Tharani (2021) states that "Wikidata is becoming a means for libraries to live institutional values, show professional solidarity, and exercise social justice." Wikidata is used by these liberation projects—it can guide, locating silences and invisibilities in the archive that need to be filled by users and policymakers alike. Yet, one can argue that the virtual assistants of large platform companies are the primary beneficiaries of projects like Wikidata (and Schema.org). But what is the future of Wikidata? Will it continue to democratize and embrace its alleged liberatory potential? Or will the project continue to consolidate and atomize knowledge in factual semantic triples whose primary purpose will be to feed media products like virtual assistants from large companies? A look into these virtual assistants will be the topic of the following chapter.

At least projects such as Wikidata are transparent compared to all the proprietary data mining activity at larger for-profit internet companies. So, in this respect, Wikidata has advantages compared to the alternatives. In the free software movement (Stallman, 2002), one might imagine a world where these large, for-profit internet companies can't suck up all of the Wikidata available without explaining what they are doing. The difficulty is that formal assertions are not copyrightable (thus, the zero copyright used by Wikidata)—the sucking up or replicability of the Wikidata becomes part of the licensing. It is true that Wikidata "feeds" facts to knowledge panels and virtual assistants. Still, it is transparent, while proprietary knowledge graphs and knowledge bases such as those described in chapter 2 are not. My critique of Wikidata and Schema.org in this book is not to exclude these larger companies from such analyses. Nor do I want to overemphasize the problems associated with open-source projects like Wikidata and Schema.org. Instead, I hope some of these discussions can open the way for researchers to receive access to study the more occluded semantic technologies that exist.

5

"An Ontology-Driven Application for the Masses"

While digital voice assistants might seem relatively new and something to which we are still becoming accustomed, the Pew Research Center found that the technology is used by "nearly half of Americans [...] mostly on their smartphones" (Pew Research Center, 2017). Virtual assistants rely on semantic technologies like those discussed in the last three chapters (knowledge graphs, Schema.org, and Wikidata). For example, in their page introducing the Schema.org structured data model, IBM indicates that Schema.org "helps developers expand their web developer skills and get a head start on advances in search engine platforms and personal assistants like Siri, Google Assistant, and Alexa" (Ogbuji, 2017). Perhaps more than the knowledge panels discussed at the beginning of this book, virtual assistants are being marketed to us as the next big transition in search.

Virtual assistants are a widely used form of ambient computing (Pedersen & Iliadis, 2020); that is, computing is happening around the human body in the environment, and their development in business contexts continues to grow. For example, Vlahos' (2019) *Talk to me: How voice computing will transform the way we live, work, and think* is a popular and business-oriented history of virtual assistants. These popular industry books do not cover how these virtual assistants depend on semantic technologies like knowledge graphs, Schema.org, and Wikidata. These technologies are primarily human-built, collaborative, and involve explicit governance and policy decisions involving various people who have different investments in the product. Even though some of these projects are technically open source, they connect to companies like Google. At the same time, they comingle with technologies such as platform knowledge graphs which are usually proprietary and completely closed off in terms of access.

Virtual assistants themselves have internal ontologies and schema vocabularies built into them to help them process information and represent knowledge. In the same way that information infrastructures like Schema.org and Wikidata create semantic categories to organize knowledge, virtual assistants have mechanisms built into them to sort information into predefined categories, which can trigger specific actions. Before getting into some of the more technical details, let's look at a few examples.

Flat Earth

Information often appears unattributed in virtual assistants, even though it comes from multiple sources beyond Wikidata and Schema.org. I should preface this part by saying that I am not a flat Earth conspiracy theorist. When I ask Alexa, "Is the Earth flat?" the response is, "In fact, the earth is not flat." Alexa supports this with information about ancient Greek philosophers and astronomers who Alexa says proved this fact, followed by more information about Ferdinand Magellan and Juan Sebastián Elcano's explorations (1519–22) that resulted in the first circumnavigation of the Earth. Alexa does not provide a source for the information, which appears to be coming directly from Alexa itself. When I ask again,

Alexa gives me information from Wikipedia. When I ask a third time, Alexa gives me another answer, stating that an "Alexa contributor" provides it. Alexa shares this information with no context or indication of its source, unlike Wikipedia. What is an "Alexa contributor," and are they an expert of some sort?

Alexa should tell you that Amazon has an "Alexa Answers" program. The program is where users can "help make Alexa smarter" by "sharing their knowledge with Alexa and the world" about "questions in categories such as Science, History, Literature, and Music." These users earn points by discovering questions that Alexa doesn't have answers for (an example they give is about "the state snack of Texas"). Several articles have reported on how "Amazon is poorly vetting Alexa's user-submitted answers" and include different incorrect or absurd answers for questions. Examples include answers to whether methane from cows affects the environment, what wine goes best with chili, if India has landed on the moon, who discovered San Francisco Bay, how to catch an elephant, and if there are zombies in Florida, along with sponsored answers from ads and spam (Wiggers, 2019). Now, of course, I'm not bringing this up because I believe in flat Earth conspiracy theories or every random factoid, but because Alexa answers are an example of the kinds of facts that companies like Amazon are beginning to present directly in search results. Virtual assistants use crowdsourced programs like these, and the semantic technologies discussed earlier.

Ambiguity

One of the main problems that virtual assistants face in answering questions correctly and helping users find information is the problem of *ambiguity*. Semantic systems catch instances of ambiguity, but many remain that are unresolved, new ones appear, and confusion can remain.

When computerized systems attempt to parse the semantic meaning of search queries, terms, and concepts, ambiguity becomes a problem for automated systems.

For example, in a book on semantic data modeling, Alexopoulos (2020) helpfully describes various types of semantic ambiguity that can occur at times (confusion of meaning when using words). These ambiguities include *phonological, syntactic, anaphoric, term-level,* and *sentence-level.* He describes phonological ambiguity as when a set of *sounds* appear the same but have a different meaning (e.g., saying sentences with homophones such as "reel" and "real" out loud). Syntactic ambiguity is when specific sentence *structures* can have different meanings depending on their design (e.g., "Who's the director that made movies with gangsters?"). Anaphoric ambiguity is when words refer to something *previous,* but there is more than one possibility of what it could be (e.g., "Leave a note that Cutter owes me money and Ollie owes me a ride, and then call them"). Term-level semantic ambiguity is when *terms* have multiple meanings (e.g., the word "set" in "Set the document on Monday"). Lastly, sentence-level semantic ambiguity is when *sentences* are left ambiguous (e.g., "Both movies are sequels"). These are just some ambiguity problems that semantic media such as virtual assistants come up against that are not always resolved.

Computer scientists and researchers have attempted to define and resolve issues around semantic ambiguity and indeterminacy for years (Ginsberg, 2008; Hayes and Halpin, 2008; Halpin et al., 2010; Poirier, 2019), and today, even on major internet platforms, issues around ambiguity are a constant challenge. For example, Google has developed metrics for determining what ambiguous words like "best" mean given a particular context—from 2015 to 2017, searches with the word "best" increased by over 80%. Google had to figure out how people "make decisions based on differences beyond quality, price, and basic features" (Wheaton, 2018). The search engine optimization blog *SEO by the Sea* has documented and explained Google patents for technologies that attempt to resolve these issues around ambiguity, including patents with titles like "Semi structured question answering system" and "Determining question and answer alternatives" (Slawski, 2019a, 2019b). These patents explain how Google tries to disambiguate when people ask questions for ambiguous things like "Washington's age" and "Harry Potter length." Companies attend to the ambiguity problem in semantic media in several ways. Some come from tools that companies develop themselves, such as specific natural language processing mechanisms found in virtual assistants, or ones they acquire, such as proprietary knowledge graphs and knowledge bases and public projects like Wikidata and Schema.org.

Virtual Assistant History

As it turns out, virtual assistants linked to semantic technologies from the beginning. "Ontology" was used intermittently in early conversations about AI, information theory, and computer science. Still, in the early 1990s, with the publication of a series of papers by Tom Gruber (1991, 1993a, 1993b, 1995), ontology spread as a popular term for achieving semantic interoperability among heterogeneous data. In his entry for "Ontology" in the *Encyclopedia of database systems*, Gruber (2009a) elaborates, writing that "in practice, the languages of ontologies are closer in expressive power to first-order logic than languages used to model databases."

For centuries a philosophical concern, ontology became a practical concern for researchers and practitioners who tried to grapple with data-driven labeling practices, including virtual assistants. In computer and information science, a metadata infrastructure of entities and descriptions of their attendant meanings, definitions, and relations is an example of a computational ontology. Guarino et al. (2009) define ontology as a "means to formally model the structure of a system, i.e., the relevant entities and relations that emerge from its observation, and which are useful" (Guarino is another early practitioner of applied ontology work and a significant figure in the field).

The same year that Gruber released his encyclopedic definition of ontology, he gave presentations about Siri based on research sponsored by the military (Gruber, 2009b). Like most things associated with foundational internet infrastructure, virtual assistants received initial funding from DARPA (recall that DARPA was also involved in initial semantic web funding). DARPA's Personalized Assistant that Learns (PAL) program funded a project called Cognitive Assistant that Learns and Organizes (CALO), which ran from 2003 to 2008. The research group that conducted CALO work was SRI International (formerly the Stanford Research Institute). Some considered CALO the Pentagon's most significant investment in artificial intelligence. Siri Inc. was a spin-off from this project in 2007 and released the virtual assistant app in 2010, which was acquired and released by Apple in 2011 as part of their mobile phone operating system—Markoff (2008) describes more of this history.

Siri

Applied ontologies are in popular social media graphs like those by Facebook and Google and virtual personal assistants like Siri. On the front-end interface, these apps and services present categories that the user can choose from—for example, social media systems encode gender in design (Bivens & Haimson, 2016) or choose types of cuisines or other inputs. Users see only an outward-facing part of proprietary ontologies, and the public does not know how companies have organized their metadata or with whom companies may share the data.

As a key figure in ontology research in information science in the 1990s, Gruber, mentioned above, was also a project lead on Siri. Siri was referred to by its creators as "an ontology-driven application for the masses" (Cheyer & Gruber, 2010). It uses something they refer to as an "Active Ontology" to build and run applications. The 2006 patent "Method and apparatus for building an intelligent automated assistant" (Cheyer & Guzzoni, 2006) describes the process. Apple's patents for Siri show diagrams of the Active Ontology at work, organizing the data from various sources by creating concepts under which they can fall. The patent titled "Intelligent automated assistant" (Gruber et al., 2010) also describes some of this work. Figure 5.1 contains figures from these patents that show the Active Ontology and how it divides and organizes data. The figure at the top shows how facts are collected and processed for execution through a flowchart. A single fact is collected at the beginning, then processed with other facts to create a rule that will execute a corresponding action in the virtual assistant. The figure at the bottom displays the Active Ontology in the center, which directs and orchestrates several components.

Siri's Active Ontology takes data provided from multiple services that the ontology orchestrates (e.g., apps like Yelp and Instagram). The product then runs them through domains and task modules (essentially, designated categories like "restaurant" and "movies") and connects them to intelligent user interfaces (what the user sees or hears). The Active Ontology connects and organizes the disparate data provided by apps (via APIs), so Siri can relate semantic or intelligent information to the user. There are other elements, of course, but the Active Ontology is the conduit through which data from the other components are passed and shaped. Other Apple patents describe ontologies for data processed in Siri from apps and data in a physical environment such as a home. For example, which room a person is in, tracked via GPS to remind that person to do something in that room when they walk into it or something to do later. Gruber has stated that "Siri is building on the ecosystem of APIs, which are better if they

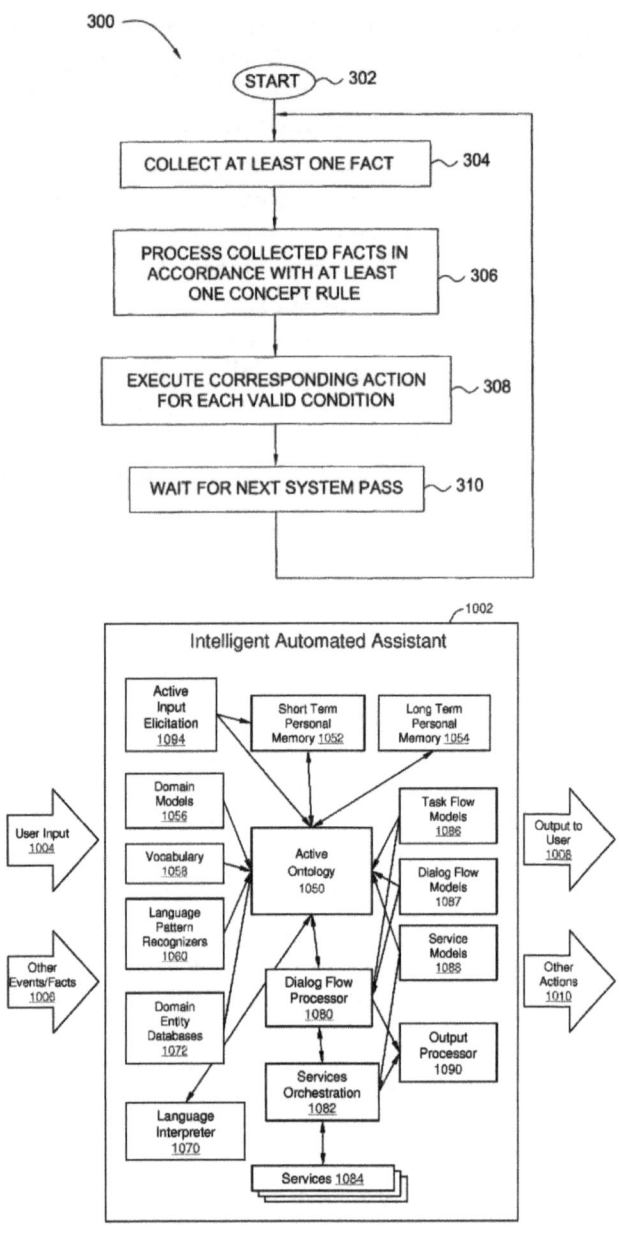

Figure 5.1: Siri's fact processing (top) described in Cheyer and Guzzoni (2006), and Active Ontology (bottom) described in Gruber et al. (2010)

declare the meaning of the data in and out via ontologies. That is the original purpose of ontologies-as-specification that I promoted in the 1990s—to help specify how to interact with these agents via knowledge-level APIs" (Spivack, 2010). Entities like Schema.org and Wikidata make these processes much more accessible. They can also easily transmit knowledge to Siri, which can further parse it, and relay that information to users.

Google Assistant

Siri was perhaps the first and best-known among virtual assistants, but several other companies now offer such assistants and have increased their market share. Google has published papers on scaling virtual assistant responses using natural language processing and a schema-guided (semantic) approach (Rastogi et al., 2020). A Google Search Central blog posting from 2018 states that, since Google launched its assistant in 2016, they have collaborated on Schema.org structured data for publishers to mark up sections of the news that are read aloud to users of the assistant (Raman, 2018). Google Assistant will often read longer content from Wikipedia, and much of the information it relates, including the simple facts that it states, comes from Wikidata.

Schemas like Schema.org and knowledge bases like Wikidata will continue to provide semantic information for companies like Google, and their use and complexity are likely to grow. John Mueller, a webmaster trends analyst at Google, has said that in the future, Google will "have more types of structured data markup, and it will continue to get more complicated" (Google Search Central, 2020). Mueller has stated that there are numerous requirements for search, particularly if people want fancy results, site highlights, or results in Google Assistant, and that "all of these things, they currently rely a lot on structured data markup." Google Assistant, thus, needs assistance with tracking down and articulating facts discerned from all the unstructured information on the internet.

Often, semantic representations such as those described throughout this book pair with more statistics-based natural language processes. In a paper titled "Semantic lattice processing in contextual automatic speech recognition for Google Assistant" (Velikovich et al., 2018), Google researchers describe "broad semantic classes comprising millions of entities, such as songs and musical artists, to tag relevant semantic entities" in Google Assistant. This approach pairs natural language techniques such as named entity recognition with semantic information for contextual automated speech recognition. The authors describe classes such as "tv_series," "tv_program," "actor," "composer," "film," etc., as well as sample instances of each of these terms. These internal processes pair with Google's Knowledge Graph. As Chah (2018) notes, "Google Assistant taps into the structured data in the proprietary Google Knowledge Graph (KG) to answer queries" and that there is an "underlying ontology that structures the Knowledge Graph and by extension the kinds of answers that Google Search or Assistant can provide."

Alexa

Amazon's virtual assistant, Alexa, uses similar semantic technologies to Siri and Google Assistant. Alexa's ties to these semantic technologies are also well documented in the popular press. In a *Wired* article titled "Inside the Alexa-friendly world of Wikidata," Simonite (2019) writes that virtual assistants "do their jobs better thanks to Wikidata, which aims to (eventually) represent everything in the universe in a way computers can understand." The article quotes Vrandečić as stating, "Language depends on knowing a lot of common sense, which computers don't have access to." Semantic schemas and ontologies thus allegedly help "bake" this common sense into these products. Virtual assistants like Alexa "do their jobs better because of Wikidata"—the companies that created them "scrape the data and combine it with other sources—though exactly how they use the information, or to what extent, hasn't been made public." Wikidata is incomplete and messy, and the article describes the roughly quarter of it that does not have references.

The ontologies in virtual assistants organize the data that they retrieve into categories. Then the speech uttered by their customers also becomes placed into categories—these are then both matched and combined. Alexa, for example, has a certain number of discrete "intents" that it recognizes. Amazon offers developers an Alexa Skills Kit that allows them to repurpose Alexa to conduct individual tasks and services like reporting the news and playing games (an API for this extension exists). Alexa can mistake vocal expressions like other virtual assistants, and the services often can't process complex queries and statements. Like Siri and Google Assistant, researchers at Amazon have developed an ontology of types, entities, properties, relationships, actions, and roles for the product. They also created the Alexa Meaning Representation Language, a graph-based meaning representation (like an ontology or a knowledge graph). The language takes the actions, operators, relations, and classes, labels them as vertices, and labels the properties and roles as edges (recall the semantic networks discussed earlier). This representation is "grounded in the Alexa ontology, which provides a common semantic representation for spoken language understanding and can directly represent ambiguity, complex nested utterances, and cross-domain queries" (Kollar et al., 2018). An example that Amazon researchers discuss is when you utter the words "play Michael Jackson's 'Thriller'" that will trigger an "ActivateAction" concerning a "MusicRecording" which the ontology can parse. Another example shows how when you say "turn on the living room light" that will also trigger an "ActivateAction" for "Lighting." Figure 5.2 shows how this process breaks down in the ontology.

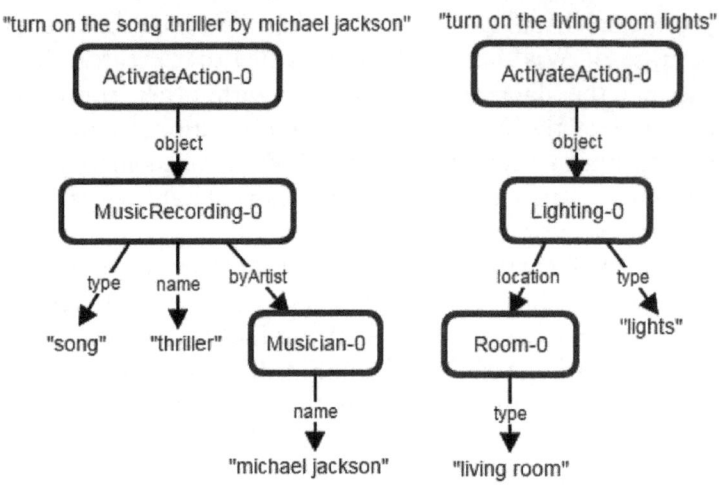

Figure 5.2: Alexa ontology breaking down statements into entities and relations

Source: Kollar et al., 2018. Licensed under CC BY 4.0.

Alexa's ontology is described as providing a "common semantics" and is "developed in RDF" (the semantic data model). The nodes are to represent classes, and the lines are properties; the root of both is the activate action. Other passages in the research describe how the ontology treats things like conjunctions, cross-domain utterances, spatial relations, and composition. Further research from Amazon describes the Alexa ontology as "a version of Schema.org [...] that has been adapted for spoken language understanding." It focuses on "fine-grained types along with actions, verb roles, and properties" (Perera et al., 2018). Abend and Rappoport (2017) describe how semantic schemas and ontologies are used in natural language processing for virtual assistants and other state-of-the-art technologies.

Virtual Assistants and Politics

There is potential for the facts represented in or through sources like Wikidata and Schema.org to contain errors or not get things right when virtual assistants utter them. Parker (2017) relates that a Reddit user discovered that Siri once thought that the hit dance song "Despacito" was the national anthem of Bulgaria (the real anthem is "Mila Rodino"). He writes that "As of this writing, if you ask Apple's voice assistant, 'What is the national anthem of Bulgaria?', you'll get the result, 'The national anthem of Bulgaria is Despacito.'" The error happened because there was a mistake in the metadata of one of the sources that the virtual assistant was consulting (probably Wikipedia or Wikidata). Thus, the virtual assistant got the facts wrong, too. But it is not only these fact sources that have the potential to convey misinformation; each assistant has its internal ontology as well, and many of them are not open to public scrutiny. We don't know the content of many categories in virtual assistants, so we don't know how often they can get things wrong.

Virtual assistants are not devoid of politics. Ojeda (2019), in a piece titled "The political responses of virtual assistants," analyzed each of the principal virtual assistants' responses to political questions and gauged their understanding of political concepts. After asking 150 technical questions, Ojeda found that virtual assistants "have an above average knowledge of politics, an elementary understanding of important political concepts, and only a handful of opinions on the matters of the day." Figure 5.3 shows how much each virtual assistant knows about institutions and processes, figures and parties, foreign and domestic affairs, history and geography, and concepts such as fairness, peace, poverty, racism, etc. The evidence shows that the subject of politics is discernible to these technologies, suggesting that such information will continue to be related to them in the future. How virtual assistants interface with semantic technologies will determine the quality of these responses.

As Siri's founders once stated, technologies like virtual assistants are ontology-driven applications for the masses. The ontologies that inform these assistants have several

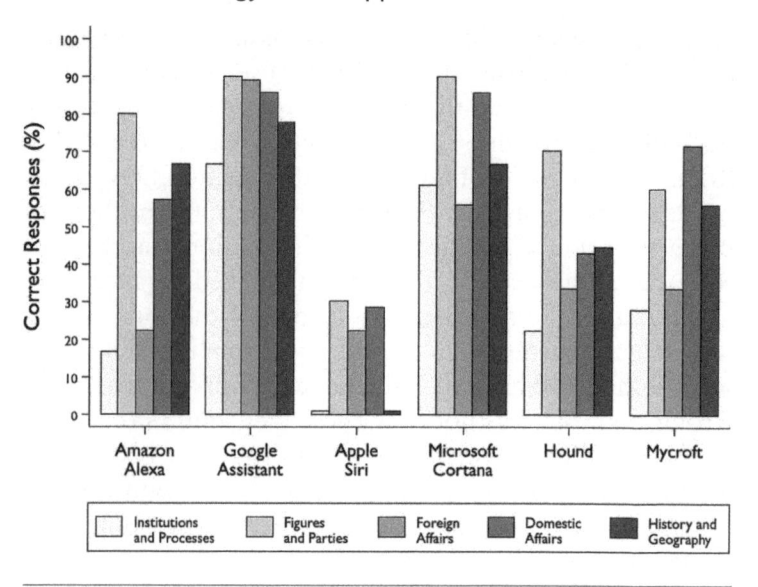

Concept	Virtual Assistants Offering a Reasonable Definition						
	Amazon's Alexa	Google Assistant	Apple's Siri	Microsoft's Cortana	Hound	Mycroft	Total
Fairness	✓	✓		✓	✓	✓	5
Peace	✓	✓		✓	✓	✓	5
Poverty	✓	✓		✓	✓	✓	5
Racism	✓	✓		✓	✓	✓	5
Arrow's theorem				✓	✓	✓	4
Power	✓	✓		✓		✓	4
Trust		✓		✓	✓	✓	4
War	✓	✓		✓		✓	4
Social contract theory		✓		✓	✓		3
Democracy		✓		✓			2
Political trust		✓		✓			2
Tragedy of the commons		✓			✓		2
Prisoner's dilemma		✓					1
Justice							0
Total	6	13	0	11	8	8	

Figure 5.3: The political responses of virtual assistants

Source: Ojeda, C. (2019). The political responses of virtual assistants. *Social Science Computer Review*, 39(5), 884–902. https://doi. org/10.1177/0894439319886844. Copyright © 2019 by SAGE. Reprinted by Permission of Sage Publications.

points where politics inform their data processing, from the underlying schemas and knowledge bases that feed them facts, to the internal organizing and labeling systems that these technologies employ, to how virtual assistants choose to relay this knowledge. Several scholars, such as Sweeney (2016a, 2016b) and Guzman (2017), have conducted studies on how issues such as gender, race, and class link to virtual assistant technologies, from their voices to the knowledge they relate. If usage statistics are correct, then the use of virtual assistants will continue to grow, as will the degree to which they are relied upon for searching for political facts and information.

Levels of Communication

Technologies like virtual assistants and others described in this book show us how communication processes occur on several informational levels. Some are technical and automated, and others are human-made and manual, but all rely on emerging forms of informational organization (Bencherki & Iliadis, 2019). Here, I do not simply mean "information" in a strictly statistical or algorithmic sense; I also mean in a symbolic and semantic understanding. There is a tendency to split the idea of communicating between *communication* as something that happens symbolically among humans as an interpersonal, group, or cultural phenomenon and *communications* as something that occurs among machines in a strictly technical sense. Instead, scholars should accept that some of what people see as human communication (semantics, meaning) happens in devices like virtual assistants and knowledge graphs. At the same time, in other domains like emerging health products, there is computing (signals, processing) happening in, on, or around the human body (Iliadis, 2020). I hope that this book is one small contribution toward breaking down this binary. New research projects in human–machine communication have already identified such changes to understand how humans interact with machines as communicative subjects (Guzman, 2018).[16] There are many opportunities for researchers from other fields such as media, science and technology studies, information, sociology, philosophy, political science, anthropology, and others, to follow and create their unique contributions to this emerging research area.

Information retrieval since the 1950s has involved some manner of connecting input from a search box to a concept (Joudrey & Taylor, 2018). This book shows how data infrastructures enable such processes in today's semantic media products. This book has discussed search practices, but its primary focus has been on the semantic theories, technologies, and media that enable searching and how these products construct, organize, and convey knowledge. While this book did not focus explicitly on the topic of people's searching practices, researchers have studied this type of interaction in the context of human information retrieval and interaction (Fidel, 2012; Sundin et al., 2017, 2022) and will continue to do so in examining the intersection of semantic search and semantic media.

Visions

The technologies described in this book align with specific visions of the world, ones where the open connectivity of facts and information is ideal. This passionate focus on what people understand as a noble cause can sometimes miss adverse effects and outcomes. Indeed, it is good to try to reduce misinformation, share knowledge, and better understand how we communicate our experiences. But the paths that we use to achieve these aims are fraught with potential missteps. The creators of media like virtual assistants want to harness the data from products like knowledge graphs, Wikidata, and Schema.org so that they can convey facts and assertions. Yet, these technologies have a way of treating the world's knowledge as something that can be isolated, organized, and distributed through industrial and global-scale media production. What does such a global source of knowledge do to local knowledge? What gets lost in translation? Who are the beneficiaries, and who gets left out of these projects? Should we continuously extract knowledge and package facts into these easily transmissible bits that large platform companies can share? Indeed, not all information benefits from extrapolation, automation, and distribution.

Several scholars have examined the importance of local data and sources of information so that we do not forget where data originate and the power that comes from taking these data for other purposes (Loukissas, 2019; D'Ignazio & Klein, 2020). Similarly, we might question when and where it becomes beneficial to share facts and information via semantic media and when it ends up causing more harm than good. Is it necessary to have global platform-controlled knowledge graphs like the one operated by Google, knowledge bases like the one represented by Wikidata, universal web schemas like Schema.org, and virtual assistants and knowledge panels that relay data from these massive projects? Must we always have global aspirations that aim to solve the Tower of Babel problem of the non-transmissibility of distributed languages and knowledge from the top down? We might focus on creating more localized data infrastructures and communities that develop models of facts, meaning, and knowledge from the bottom up. Though they maintain a universalist ambition, the media technologies described in this book cannot use models to fully represent a reality that will always exceed them.

At the same time, more local projects that take advantage of these semantic technologies seem possible as a space to harness the power of small groups of experts. Their knowledge may overlap to provide or work toward producing alternatives to more totalizing or top-down approaches to knowledge sharing. At a practical level, open-source and publicly available semantic technologies help connect data across domains and make it easier for people to work with public data. Such projects include those coming from governments and other sources where public scrutiny and sharing of such data is of utmost importance for public safety, oversight, and reform. Such small groups and projects happen all the time, while larger companies that view scale and portability as necessary may wonder why such groups bother.

A Plea for Access

Readers will have noticed that two of the case studies in this book were on open-source technologies (Schema. org and Wikidata). While I think it is essential to be critical even of technologies that purport to be open and for the public good, I do not want their critiques to overshadow the more fundamental analyses of the large media companies. Google, Facebook, Microsoft, Amazon, etc., all have semantic technologies they use for semantic media products, which also use the open-source products mentioned above. Unlike open-source projects, researchers do not have access to these technologies, so there is limited opportunity to study them critically. Researchers must access these semantic technologies to review them and their applications. Most of this book would have aimed at those technologies rather than a single chapter (chapter 2) if such access had been available.

Knowledge graphs like the one operated by Google are proprietary and not open the way that Schema.org and Wikidata are. The majority of knowledge graphs described in this book are the private intellectual property of internet companies. Such knowledge graphs are in pharmaceutical companies, defense contractors, and enterprise knowledge management. So there are different types of closed knowledge graphs, and researchers need access to them. One of the reasons is that it is difficult to gauge how open projects like Wikidata and Schema.org feed into them. Since Google's Knowledge Graph is opaque, we do not know the extent of its data gathering, even though data from such sources end up in the knowledge panels and virtual assistants that communicate facts.

A Farewell to Facts?

Many crises are unfolding across the internet today, ranging from misinformation and conspiracies about things such as elections and vaccines. Misinformation has been on the rise after the 2016 US presidential election and again since the COVID-19 pandemic. One might wonder whether or not we are in need, now more than ever, of specific facts upon which we all agree and that can be transmitted automatically across media systems. We live in an era where some desire not to take things at face value, misrepresent opponents, and weaponize and manipulate information. Is there not some sense that we need mechanisms for distributing common facts that are believable and shared?

Defining what constitutes a "fact" is an old problem. In *A history of the modern fact: Problems of knowledge in the sciences of wealth and society* (1998), Mary Poovey describes that understanding the formal semantic systems in which facts transmit becomes, in some sense, more important than the facts themselves for understanding how we receive specific facts. Here she means systems like mathematical tables, bookkeeping, and other formalized representations of information throughout history. To this list, we might add the semantic triples that feed into the semantic media that represent facts in today's mediated world. When we speak about "facts," are we talking about formalized assertions such as the type enabled by the technologies discussed in this book, or do we do so in a more general and philosophical sense? Are there moments where it becomes appropriate that some institution or group of people comes to think more globally, seeking to connect facts with a universalizing eye technologically, and others where it is more appropriate to maintain a local approach? The "scalability" of facts may be preferred when media systems require generalizability. In other cases, it might be more advantageous to seek a diversity of systems that are not interoperable across the internet. The answer to these questions, I think, depends on the context. It also depends on deliberation and who is allowed a seat at the table.

Conclusion

Ontology-driven media technologies like Google and Facebook's graphs, popular semantic web standards, and virtual assistants like Siri, Google Assistant, and Alexa provide many opportunities for transmitting facts and meanings instantaneously without leading people to other sources. But, like any technology, they can impede social progress if, during their development, designers are not also attentive to data and design justice issues (Dencik et al., 2016; Costanza-Chock, 2020). Semantic media present truly unique problems—they are not only a matter of quantification but also a matter of meaning. How are social entities and relations defined? What languages do ontologies recognize? We are already well on our way to a semantic, "intelligent," and "intuitive" internet that presumes to know what we mean. It is time to start thinking ahead of the technology, improve social institutions, help vulnerable communities, and focus less on profit and efficiency.

Companies that release semantic media products engage in social ontology (Krämer & Conrad, 2017; Iliadis, 2018) by building facts and meanings about social entities into their products. Such is an example of what

Langlois (2014) has called automated "ways of producing meaning." Semantic media will likely evolve beyond things like knowledge panels and virtual assistants to include augmented and virtual reality forms of embodied computing that can relay semantically augmented information about people, places, and things. Indeed, there is already much technical research and development in combining a virtual assistant with augmented reality devices. Something like your glasses will identify things, pull up relevant facts and information, and then tell you what they are. Emerging media technologies directly tell us about facts, meanings, and stories, and they signal the beginning of a relatively new era of media. Social and critically minded researchers are also already beginning to investigate semantic media from the perspective of the everyday people that interact with these technologies (Halford et al., 2013).

Returning to the Politics of Search

The history of search is not new, and there have been several books and hundreds of articles about how search has changed with the introduction of new media products from internet companies. Specifically, the classic work by Introna and Nissenbaum (2000) addressed how "search engines raise not merely technical issues but also political ones" by excluding "certain sites and certain types of sites in favor of others, systematically giving prominence to some at the expense of others." Their work addressed search engines' biases concerning the ordering of links as sources for users to browse. Legal scholars have been attentive to the consequences of search bias (Grimmelmann, 2007, 2009, 2014). I argue that we've entered the next era of political search. What is at stake is not just ordered results as a list of links but the meaning of the facts provided directly by internet companies (in organized panels, menus, or audio answers).

One of the first book-length critical studies about search engines was Halavais' *Search engine society* (2008/2017). The book raised several themes relevant to the semantic media covered in this book, including what was, at the time, emerging discussion around things such as semantic technologies and the history of semantics on the web. The book deals with central search themes, such as how attention and knowledge are changing with the advancements of search engines. Halavais remarks in the book that, at the time, the notion of pulling structured data from the primarily unstructured data on the web seemed promising and that web administrators wishing to be recognized by search engines typically included metadata in their pages. In detailing the important changing features of search and hinting at search's semantic future, Halavais (2008/2017) remains a critical text that identified the horizon of emerging semantic media that were to come in popular internet products. Further scholars have examined the political implications of search, including DeNardis (2009) on the politics of internet infrastructure and governance and Golumbia (2009) on the capitalist cultural influences of computation.

Another of the earliest and sustained critiques of platform companies' attempts to monopolize search while also forecasting the current emphasis on semantics is Vaidhyanathan's *The Googlization of everything* (2011). Vaidhyanathan writes that companies such as Google did not, at the time, try to read and understand the meaning of search queries. Yet, tech companies were already working to develop technologies capable of semantic search to incorporate and understand the contexts and intentions of things identified in search terms entered by users. For example, Vaidhyanathan explains that entering strings of text like "What is the capital of [x]?" in earlier search engines would result in links that directed users to sources where that exact text string is present. Vaidhyanathan, like Halavais, noted that a "semantic search" engine that reads and understands natural language would provide a meaningful answer to the user's query rather than produce a list of matching strings of words. Apart from the technical, semantic aspects discussed in the text, Vaidhyanathan's notion of "infrastructural imperialism" presented in the book was an early critique of Google's use of infrastructure to expand its hegemonic cultural power (through Google Books, etc.). Vaidhyanathan, like Halavais, points to this new emerging era of web power in terms of semantics, where internet companies can decipher and convey meaning directly to web users.[17]

More recently, three book-length studies on knowledge and representation in search—Noble's (2018) *Algorithms of oppression*, Thomas' (2018) *Becoming-social in a networked age*, and Haider and Sundin's (2019) *Invisible search and online search engines*—round out this book's influences. Noble (2018) focuses on the sociocultural biases in search results (such as stereotypes depicted in Google Images when searching for specific racial or gender terms). The book influenced my understanding of how semantic media are never neutral and are always susceptible to presenting limited knowledge when answering queries. Noble's book asks readers to think about what counts as the "best" information and, more importantly, for "whom?" Thomas (2018) pulls in a slightly different direction, focusing on the semantic nature of contemporary internet media technologies that often conduct some naming and classifying of entities for easy uptake in search infrastructures. Thomas' book asks critical epistemological questions about what happens when "knowledge" is expressed through a graph's logical data relations. The book interrogates the philosophical and historical nature of knowledge graphs and what they mean in terms of social relations and how we think about epistemology and theories of knowledge. Lastly, Haider and Sundin (2019) is a comprehensive and critical account of the power of search engines today. The book points to works of scholarship in information search and behavior, highlighting the often overlooked (by casual users) ways that search engines operate.

Finally, I would be remiss not to mention a few classic works on the political economy of communication that informed this book. Innis' (1951) *The Bias of Communication* focuses on biases and power and argues that modern communication technologies undermine conceptions of space, time, and place. Smythe's (1977) work on critical approaches to communication and Mosco's (1996/2009) *The political economy of communication* also aided my thinking about the consequences of media ownership in an era of automated semantics and the internet, as did Fuchs' (2009) and Winseck's (2017) work on the political economy of internet infrastructure. I am interested in the political economy of how data infrastructures and the technologies, organizations, and processes that support them are organized to enable automated knowledge representation on the internet. Thus, I also drew from work in the politics of knowledge representation and organization in information systems and critical data studies (Bowker & Star, 1999; Day, 2000, 2001; Olson, 2001, 2002; Duarte & Belarde-Lewis, 2015; Burns et al., 2018; Iliadis & Russo, 2016; Leazer & Montoya, 2020; Littletree et al., 2020).

As I stated at the beginning of this conclusion, the politics of search is nothing new. DiMaggio et al. (2001) and Hargittai (2007) focused on the social implications of how search engines represent and organize content. Decades ago, they explained that scholars must understand these technologies and their sociocultural biases for social progress—for example, Gerhart (2004) found that searches for information typically present positive results. Other scholars articulated research programs to examine that new and emerging area. Rieder (2005) made several recommendations relevant to search engines, including that researchers should focus on data in terms of its scope, structure, relevance, and how it is extracted, along with a focus on its representation and how results are present. In another study, Rieder (2009) explored this area, isolating how the web functions as a set of links and documents and noting that search engines, at the time, were primarily based on keyword searches (a practice different from how we as humans understand and order information in categories and contexts). At the time, Reider noted that search engines had a "relative agnosticism to meaning" in favor of a cultural logic of objectivity. Indeed, around the same time, Golumbia (2009) commented on Google's lack of ability to search for the semantics of items on individual pages outside of simple keyword searches.

The situation is remarkably different now, with the addition of products in search that focus explicitly on semantics and meaning rather than keywords. In 2019, my colleague Amelia Acker and I organized a series of panels at the Society for Social Studies of Science conference in New Orleans. Acker is currently an Associate Professor in the School of Information at the University of Texas at Austin, where she directs the Critical Data Studies Lab. The meetings were called "Schemas, graphs, ontologies: Baking semantics into data-driven media technologies." There, we convened a group of researchers (many of whom are cited in this book) who were interested in studying some of the topics that appear in this book from political economy and sociological perspectives, ranging from RDF and the W3C to Wikidata, Schema.org, expert systems, applied ontologies, and how platform companies are using these technologies today. We invited senior scholars and graduate students who gave a variety of presentations. Our reason for organizing the event was that we thought that these necessary media technologies were not being given enough attention by socially and critically minded researchers in fields like media and communication.

A presentation by one of our attendees, Golden (2019), commented on the hegemony of products like Schema.org. He stated that one of the fundamental reasons that scholars should study products like Schema.org was that it is "endorsed by the world's major search engines at a time when a user's quest for information is more likely to begin on the broader Web than in a library or even a library website." Golden makes an interesting point— what will happen when everyone begins their search for information not at a library or even the regular version of Wikipedia but only on search engines or virtual assistants with their knowledge graphs and schemas? With this and other considerations around knowledge monopolization, cultural hegemony, and the political economy of communication in mind, I offer several theses in conclusion.

Five Theses

I have tried to argue that semantic media represent a relatively significant shift to technologies that convey facts, answers, meanings, and "knowledge" directly to people in media products. I've also tried to provide context concerning these semantic media's social and political ramifications. There are several reasons why we should be concerned about how semantic media will continue to develop.

1. *While semantic media allow people to look up facts more efficiently, they are also in danger of eliminating verifiability.* As semantic media continue to offer up answers for their users, they erase opportunities for people to verify the facts presented to them. When companies give information about people, places, processes, relationships, and things, they seldom provide details for verifying the data. If these trends continue, we will eventually live in a world where we cite Google and Amazon as official sources to demonstrate knowledge. We will depend on the often inaccurate technologies of for-profit companies. This type of confirmation is a dangerous path to head down for reasons associated with conflict of interest, financial incentives, and sociocultural biases ignored in favor of profits. New products by internet companies are a popular way to receive facts and knowledge, especially among young

people, even though their verifiability is not up to a high standard.

2. *While semantic media promote sharing knowledge, they are in danger of consolidating the world's knowledge and drowning out local knowledge by monopolizing meaning.* Internet companies' information is from numerous sources and places to create maximum efficiency and produce a less scattered, more centralized set of knowledge upon which to draw. This type of consolidation of knowledge has implicit effects, such as diminishing the robustness and detail of heterogeneous expertise or knowledge that may not fit the mold or logic of the centralizing agency. Facts and knowledge become stripped down and shaped according to the sense of whatever consolidating power appropriates and repackages it; this may be due to such things as space limitations, capacity to represent specific types of knowledge, or archiving biases. Scholars such as Knorr Cetina (1999) have examined the *epistemic cultures* that form and give rise to such knowledge creation: cultures that shape and influence what, when, where, why, and how knowledge exists, or cultures that "create and warrant knowledge." Scholars such as Fricker (2007) have explained how the cultural construction of such knowledge may lead to *epistemic injustice*, that is, injustices "done to someone specifically in their capacity as a knower." What will happen to those whose knowledge exists outside the graphs and panels— will their knowledge be deemed worthy? Such injustices may take the form of individual prejudices that limit the credibility of an individual's knowledge or structural biases that prevent certain concepts and understanding.

3. *While semantic media share much collaboratively sourced information, they are in danger of being parasitic upon and exploiting social data.* How will the social facts that media companies present through their technologies change the political economy of knowledge? Following Wihbey (2019), I view social facts as "media content accompanied and influenced by information indicating

social attention or approval [...] they are data used to drive what becomes public knowledge." Semantic media rely on social attention, such as structured web data produced on collaborative sites or markup, and more extensive resources such as open databases. Semantic media take out the content of those social sources and then repackage and repurpose it on their products. This process has the effect of driving down traffic to those sites, creating less revenue, and impacting their business models. It also shows that semantic media rely on social facts that themselves are prone to inaccuracies. In this way, semantic media are a kind of vampire that extracts knowledge as social facts from smaller or open-sourced operations, using this data to strengthen their products and services. Eventually, the smaller pages that offer these facts will die, losing traffic and resources, and the larger internet companies will survive thanks to their sacrifice. That internet companies exploit the data of regular internet users has been well documented and continues to be a significant research area (Elmer, 2003; Couldry & Mejías, 2019), particularly in the realm of data modeling and knowledge representation in information systems.

4. *While semantic media may present facts that are, in some cases, democratically sourced, they also create new gatekeepers to knowledge.* Scholars have always discussed large internet companies as new types of gatekeepers, typically in news contexts. For example, Google privileges certain websites in their list of links using a ranking system, affecting journalism and the news industry regarding what sources reach the most people (Wallace, 2018). News is now also becoming automated on platforms like Google and Facebook. Their algorithms "surface, filter, highlight, and disseminate information" that "can make the difference in whether important civic stories are heard and reach critical mass" (Diakopoulos, 2019). Coddington (2019) notes that such technologies also promote news aggregation by "taking news from published sources, reshaping it, and republishing it in an abbreviated form

within a single place." With semantic media, gatekeeping functions become entrenched in yet another way. Social and technological decisions come to bear on what types of facts or knowledge count and how news media show them. Standards, committees, technologies, and processes determine how these semantics are orchestrated and are often not discernible to the public. Who or what can produce this information, who sits on steering committees, and what people are involved? There are questions about governance, political economy, and control, mainly where companies source the facts that populate their semantic media.

5. *While semantic media may seemingly offer neutral results, they are in danger of typifying logic, sociocultural biases, and misinformation.* The information presented in semantic media products will often show specific logic or preferences concerning the information they contain and how the media represents and displays it, just as the original keyword search results always returned socio-politically biased results (Diaz, 2008; Goldman, 2005). Such has been well known in search communities for some time. Yet, the exposure to such political biases in terms of knowledge representation in semantic media creates further opportunities to research and examine them. Drawing on work in search and older work in knowledge representation technologies, scholars may study these issues with large web-based media products transmitting knowledge at scale. While scholars have continuously researched political bias in search results and websites like Wikipedia almost since their inception, scholars are also now turning to examine data structures pulled from knowledge representations in data infrastructures like Wikidata—see the work of the Whose Knowledge? project (Vrana et al., 2020), Tripodi (2021) on gender bias in Wikipedia, and Gebru et al. (2021) on biases in widely used datasets that inform things like machine learning.

Large companies have a significant stake in knowledge bases, and their power in manipulating that knowledge is great. Just as media technology companies have traditionally altered information in things like online maps and search results based on what country you are in, they can and will do the same with the "knowledge" conveyed by their products. We should expect nothing less from these companies when relating "knowledge" and facts. What's to stop them from editing and manipulating facts when it suits them? How will facts be distributed across borders and geographic locations? These are the types of questions that we should begin to think about in the study of semantic media.

What comes next for researchers and critics of semantic media, and where should they look? Immediate areas that come to mind are knowledge panels, their iterations, and virtual assistant responses. Researchers are already beginning to test question and answering devices. But there are also plenty of valuable insights from the first generation of search engine research that have lasted and others we can reimagine for current projects. A continued critical focus on semantic media products and their contexts and embodied representations will shape future conceptualizations of mediated facts and their construction.

The increasing semanticization of media is visible in how media products respond to questions about people and places. Proprietary knowledge graphs owned by private companies and open web schemas and knowledge bases help companies transmit facts in richly curated results. This information can omit or obscure the whole meaning of the topics they are supposed to represent because of decisions concerning the inclusion, presentation, and modification of information. In contexts such as the COVID-19 pandemic and information about specific conspiracy theories, such semantic media may be welcome to help push back against growing misinformation. Yet, in other contexts, the semanticization of media may potentially contribute to the distortion, or at least the truncation, of meaning. We have seen the adverse effects when 280 characters on Twitter define public communication. We know what kinds of bad outcomes and weaponization accompany this form of compact messaging. We can expect similar results from semantic media meant to automate the transmission of facts.

Facts have politics, ontology, and epistemology many of us agree on, while others we rightfully debate. We have seen the consequences of asking media companies to moderate themselves regarding the kind of content they allow on their platforms. The result is a mess, composed of uneven enforcement of rules, the continued spread of misinformation, and the inability to stop bad actors. Likewise, we can expect less than stellar results if we leave the transmission of facts to those same media companies. As social media crises around misinformation have already shown, such companies are not proactive in stopping wrong, harmful, or weaponized information if it does not immediately benefit them and their profits. They continually need to be forced to acknowledge these activities and their effects. We, then, can be proactive in demanding attention to semantic media and semanticization of facts across automated systems. Suppose we are not vigilant? In that case, we will be open to the harmful consequences of these companies' false commitments to perceived neutrality, objectivity, and impartiality. We should expect powerful media companies to act as though these ideals exist as we remain committed to questioning their universalizing aspirations.

Notes

1 As of this writing, roughly half the world's population is connected to the internet (Roser et al., 2015). I'd like to acknowledge here that this book does not assume that everyone has an internet connection, or that everyone has a high degree of computer literacy. This book is written in an informal style, so while I may refer to "people," "we," "users," "everyone," etc., I am doing so for the sake of readability—it is clear to me that many of us are privileged financially, socially, and technologically, and that large populations do not have many of these same privileges.

2 By "platforms" I mean internet-based technologies created by media companies that enable other technologies, processes, and communications to develop. For literature on platforms, see van Dijck et al. (2018). See also Gillespie (2010).

3 By media "products" I mean media that offer everyday internet users querying experiences with data-driven results. In other parts of this book, I use "product" in a simple technical sense as something that is produced. When referring to devices and things we use in our everyday searches, I use the term "media product" and I reserve "product" for generic technical description.

4 Let me pause here to say that I expect some nationalistic vitriol for including this example at the beginning of this

book (ethnocentricity being what it is). For any distraught readers who may question the once-Slav Macedonian status of the village, the University of California, Riverside's California Digital Newspaper Collection contains reports from the *Los Angeles Herald* about atrocities that occurred in the Slavic Macedonian village of Armensko (not Alona) in 1903. See also Kostopoulos (2022).

5 For more on the politics of temporality in contemporary societies, see Sharma (2014). See also Paris (2021).

6 Researchers have examined the power to name in archiving and library and information science. See Olson (2002).

7 See also van Couvering (2008) and Graham (2014).

8 Following Feinberg (2007), I do not think it is possible to avoid hidden bias in information systems entirely. Everyone and everything have certain biases. But this should not prevent us from calling out when there is a significant socio-cultural slant or orientation when it comes to technological systems whose designers often purport them to be objective and neutral. When I use the term "bias" in this book, I do so to point out significant social and cultural focus or framing in semantic media and to call for an awareness of responsibility. For more on the history of bias in technological systems, see Hoffmann (2019) and Friedman and Nissenbaum (1996).

9 For more on semiotics, see Chandler (2022).

10 The importance of semantics in philosophy marks the field's entire history. For an overview, see Coffa (1991).

11 Mackenzie (2017) offers a critical overview of the cultural and philosophical significance of machine learning, including its material instantiation of knowledge production.

12 See Thomer and Wickett (2020) for more on the materiality of databases.

13 See https://schema.org/docs/faq.html.

14 Recently, the BFO upper-level ontology became an official standard with the International Organization for Standardization (ISO) under the code ISO/IEC 21838. This standard is a multipart standard; parts one and two have been released, and others are in development. See Arp et al. (2015) for more information about BFO.

15 See Whose Knowledge? (2022).

16 For more, see Iliadis (2022).

17 The technologies discussed in this book pick up these
   threads by Vaidhyanathan (2011) and Halavais (2008/2017)
   and discuss the widening semantic era of search. Further
   relevant literature in the early stages of search studies
   includes *Google and the myth of universal knowledge*
   (Jeanneney, 2006) and the edited collections *Web search:
   Multidisciplinary perspectives* (Spink & Zimmer, 2008) and
   Deep search: The politics of search beyond Google (Becker
   & Stalder, 2009). There is also *Google and the culture of
   search* (Hillis et al., 2012) and *Society of the query reader:
   Reflections on web search* (König & Rasch, 2014), all of
   which also aided my thinking in writing this book. Other
   critical search scholars have included Zimmer (2010) on
   web search, Granka (2010) on the politics of search, Feuz
   et al. (2011) and Mager (2012) on capitalism's influence
   on search, Ford and Graham (2016a, 2016b) on how the
   semantics of search engines represents geographic locations,
   Hui's (2016) examination of the history and philosophy of
   digital objects for computational knowledge representation,
   Waller's (2016) critique of semantic search, Thornton's
   (2017, 2018) work on linguistic capitalism, Floridi (2018)
   on semantic capitalism, Allhutter (2019) on the politics of
   semantic infrastructures, and Sundin et al.'s (2022) work on
   the relevance of search results.

References

Abbas, J. (2010). *Structures for organizing knowledge: Exploring taxonomies, ontologies, and other schema.* ALA Neal-Schuman.

Abend, O., & Rappoport, A. (2017). The state of the art in semantic representation. In R. Barzilay & M-Y. Kan (Eds.), *Proceedings of the 55th Annual Meeting of the Association for Computational Linguistics (Volume 1: Long Papers)* (pp. 77–89). ACL.

Abrams, R. (2017, December 16). Google thinks I'm dead (I know otherwise.). *The New York Times.* https://www.nytimes.com/2017/12/16/business/google-thinks-im-dead.html

Acker, A. (2015). Toward a hermeneutics of data. *IEEE Annals of the History of Computing, 37*(3), 70–5. https://doi.org/10.1109/MAHC.2015.68

Adair, B. (2020, December). The future of fact-checking is all about structured data. *NiemanLab.* https://www.niemanlab.org/2020/12/the-future-of-fact-checking-is-all-about-structured-data/

Aggarwal, N., Shekarpour, S., Bhatia, S., & Sheth, A. (2017). Knowledge graphs: In theory and practice. *CIKM '17: Proceedings of the 2017 ACM on Conference*

on *Information and Knowledge Management*. http://
sumitbhatia.net/papers/KG_Tutorial_CIKM17_part1.pdf

Alexopoulos, P. (2020). *Semantic modeling for data*. O'Reilly.

Allemang, D., Hendler, J., & Gandon, F. (2020). *Semantic web for the working ontologist: Effective modeling for linked data, RDFS, and OWL*. ACM Books. https://doi .org/10.1145/3382097

Allhutter, D. (2019). Of "working ontologists" and "high-quality human components": The politics of semantic infrastructures. In D. Ribes & J. Vertesi (Eds.), *DigitalSTS: A field guide for science & technology studies*. Princeton University Press.

Amerland, D. (2013). *Google semantic search: Search engine optimization (SEO) techniques that get your company more traffic, increase brand impact, and amplify your online presence*. Que Publishing.

Anadiotis, A.-C., Balalau, O., Conceicao, C., Galhardas, H., Haddad, M. Y., Manolescu, I., Merabi, T., & You, J. (2022). Graph integration of structured, semistructured and unstructured data for data journalism. *Information Systems*, 104, 101846. https://doi.org/10.1016/j.is.2021 .101846

Andrews, M. C. (2020a, August 9). *Time to end Google's domination of schema.org*. Story Needle. https:// storyneedle.com/time-to-end-googles-domination-of -schema-org/

Andrews, M. C. (2020b, August 23). *Who benefits from schema.org?*. Story Needle. https://storyneedle.com /who-benefits-from-schema-org/

Antoniou, G., Groth, P., Van Harmelen, F., & Hoekstra, R. (2012). *A semantic web primer*. MIT Press.

Arp, R., Smith, B., & Spear, A. D. (2015). *Building ontologies with Basic Formal Ontology*. MIT Press.

Arrington, M. (2011, May 3). *Google dissolves Search group internally, now called "Knowledge."* TechCrunch. https://techcrunch.com/2011/05/03/google-dissolves -search-group-internally-now-called-knowledge/

Auer, S., Bizer, C., Kobilarov, G., Lehmann, J., Cyganiak, R., & Ives, Z. (2007). Dbpedia: A nucleus for a web of open data. In K. Aberer et al. (Eds.), *The Semantic Web. ISWC 2007, ASWC 2007* (pp. 722–35). Springer. https://doi.org/10.1007/978-3-540-76298-0_52

Ayers, P., Matthews, C., & Yates, B. (2008). *How Wikipedia works: And how you can be a part of it.* No Starch Press.

Baca, M. (Ed.). (2016). *Introduction to metadata* (3rd ed.). Getty Research Institute.

Bagdikian, B. H. (1983/2004). *The new media monopoly: A completely revised and updated edition with seven new chapters.* Beacon Press.

Balog, K. (2018). *Entity-orientated search.* Springer.

Barysevich, A. (2021, July 29). *Semantic search: What it is & why it matters for SEO today.* Search Engine Journal. https://www.searchenginejournal.com/semantic-search-seo/264037/

Bastian, M., Heymann, S., & Jacomy, M. (2009). Gephi: An open source software for exploring and manipulating networks. *Proceedings of the International AAAI Conference on Web and Social Media, 3*(1), 361–2. https://ojs.aaai.org/index.php/ICWSM/article/view/13937

Bates, J., Lin, Y.-W., & Goodale, P. (2016). Data journeys: Capturing the socio-material constitution of data objects and flows. *Big Data & Society, 3*(2). https://doi.org/10.1177/2053951716654502

Battaglia, P. W., Hamrick, J. B., Bapst, V., Sanchez-Gonzalez, A., Zambaldi, V., Malinowski, M., ... Faulkner, R. (2018). Relational inductive biases, deep learning, and graph networks. https://arxiv.org/abs/1806.01261

Battelle, J. (2006). *The search: How Google and its rivals rewrote the rules of business and transformed our culture.* Portfolio.

Becker, K., & Stalder, F. (Eds.). (2009). *Deep search: The politics of search beyond Google.* StudienVerlag.

Bencherki, N., & Iliadis, A. (2019). The constitution of organization as informational individuation. *Communication Theory*, *31*(3), 442–62. https://doi.org/10.1093/ct/qtz018

Bender, E. M., Gebru, T., McMillan-Major, A., & Shmitchell, S. (2021). On the dangers of stochastic parrots: Can language models be too big? *FAccT '21: Proceedings of the 2021 ACM Conference on Fairness, Accountability, and Transparency* (pp. 610–23). https://doi.org/10.1145/3442188.3445922

Bergman, M. K. (2018). *A knowledge representation practionary*. Springer. https://doi.org/10.1007/978-3-319-98092-8

Berners-Lee, T. (2006, July 27). *Linked data*. W3C. https://www.w3.org/DesignIssues/LinkedData.html

Berners-Lee, T., & Fischetti, M. (1999). *Weaving the web: The original design and ultimate destiny of the world wide web*. Harper Business.

Berners-Lee, T., Hendler, J., & Lassila, O. (2001, May 1). The semantic web. *Scientific American*. https://www.scientificamerican.com/article/the-semantic-web/

Bivens, R., & Haimson, O. L. (2016). Baking gender into social media design: How platforms shape categories for users and advertisers: *Social Media + Society*, *2*(4). https://doi.org/10.1177/2056305116672486

Blass, A., Gurevich, Y., & Hudis, E. (2007). The tower-of-babel problem, and security assessment sharing. *Bulletin of European Association for Theoretical Computer Science*, *101*, 161–82.

Blondel, V. D., Guillaume, J. L., Lambiotte, R., & Lefebvre, E. (2008). Fast unfolding of communities in large networks. *Journal of Statistical Mechanics: Theory and Experiment*, (10). https://iopscience.iop.org/article/10.1088/1742-5468/2008/10/P10008

Bowker, G. C., & Star, S. L. (1999). *Sorting things out: Classification and its consequences*. MIT Press.

Bowker, G. C., Baker, K., Millerand, F., & Ribes, D. (2009). Toward information infrastructure studies: Ways of knowing in a networked environment. In: J. Hunsinger, L. Klastrup, & M. Allen (Eds.), *International handbook of internet research*. Springer. https://doi.org/10.1007 /978-1-4020-9789-8_5

Brasileiro, F., Almeida, J. P. A., Carvalho, V. A., & Guizzardi, G. (2016). Applying a multi-level modeling theory to assess taxonomic hierarchies in Wikidata. In *Proceedings of the 25th International Conference Companion on World Wide Web* (pp. 975–80). https:// doi.org/10.1145/2872518.2891117

Bray, T., Paoli, J., Sperberg-Mcqueen, C. M., Maler, E., & Yergeau, F. (1997). Extensible markup language (XML). *World Wide Web Journal*, 2(4), 29–66.

Bréal, M. (1897). *Essai de sémantique*. Hachette.

Brickley, D. (2019, August 12). *Schema.org hierarchy sunburst*. Bl.ocks. http://bl.ocks.org/danbri/1c121ea8bd 2189cf411c

Brickley, D., & Guha, R. V. (1999, March 3). *Resource description framework (RDF) schema specification*. W3C. https://www.w3.org/TR/1999/PR-rdf-schema -19990303/

Brickley, D., & Miller, L. (2014). *FOAF Vocabulary Specification 0.99*. Xmlns. http://xmlns.com/foaf/spec/

Brin, S. (1999). Extracting patterns and relations from the World Wide Web. In P. Atzeni, A. Mendelzon, & G. Mecca (Eds.), *The World Wide Web and databases* (pp. 172–83). Springer. https://doi.org/10.1007/10704656 _11

Brin, S., & Page, L. (1998a). The anatomy of a large-scale hypertextual web search engine. *International World-Wide Web Conference (WWW 1998)*.

Brin, S., & Page, L. (1998b). The anatomy of a large-scale hypertextual Web search engine. *Computer Networks and ISDN Systems*, 30(1–7), 107–17. https://doi.org/10 .1016/S0169-7552(98)00110-X

Broder, A. (2002). A taxonomy of web search. *ACM SIGIR Forum*, 36(2), 3–10.

Brown, T. B., Mann, B., Ryder, N., Subbiah, M., Kaplan,

J., Dhariwal, P., … Amodei, D. (2020). Language models are few-shot learners. *Advances in Neural Information Processing Systems*. https://arxiv.org/abs/2005.14165v4

Bruckman, A. S. (2022). *Should you believe Wikipedia? Online communities and the construction of knowledge.* Cambridge University Press.

Bucher, T. (2012a). A technicity of attention: How software "makes sense." *Culture Machine*, *13*, 1–23. https://culturemachine.net/wp-content/uploads/2019/01/470-993-1-PB.pdf

Bucher, T. (2012b). The friendship assemblage: Investigating programmed sociality on Facebook. *Television & New Media*, *14*(6), 479–93. https://doi.org/10.1177/1527476412452800

Bucher, T. (2021). *Facebook*. Polity.

Buckland, M. (1991). *Information and information systems*. Praeger.

Burns, R., Hawkins, B., Hoffmann, A. L., Iliadis, A., & Thatcher, J. (2018). Transdisciplinary approaches to critical data studies. *Proceedings of the Association for Information Science and Technology*, *55*(1), 657–60. https://doi.org/10.1002/pra2.2018.14505501074

Calaresu, M., & Shiri, A. (2015). Understanding Semantic web: A conceptual model. *Library Review*, *64*(1–2), 82–100. https://doi.org/10.1108/LR-09-2014-0097

Carnap, R. (1950/2011). Empiricism, semantics, and ontology. In R. B. Talisse & S. F. Aikin (Eds.), *The pragmatism reader: From Peirce through the present* (pp. 249–64). Princeton University Press.

Carnap, R., & Bar-Hillel, Y. (1952). *An outline of a theory of semantic information*. MIT Technical Report. https://dspace.mit.edu/bitstream/handle/1721.1/4821/RLE-TR-247-03150899.pdf

Chah, N. (2017). Freebase-triples: A methodology for processing the freebase data dumps. https://arxiv.org/abs/1712.08707

Chah, N. (2018). OK Google, what is your ontology? Or: Exploring Freebase classification to understand

Google's Knowledge Graph. https://arxiv.org/abs/1805.03885

Chandler, D. (2022). *Semiotics: The basics* (4th ed.). Routledge.

Chang, S. (2018, September 4). *Scaling knowledge access and retrieval at airbnb*. The Airbnb Tech Blog. https://medium.com/airbnb-engineering/scaling-knowledge-access-and-retrieval-at-airbnb-665b6ba21e95

Chari, S., Gruen, D. M., Seneviratne, O., & McGuinness, D. L. (2020a). Directions of explainable knowledge-enabled systems. In I. Tiddi, F. Lécué, & P. Hitzler (Eds.), *Knowledge graphs for eXplainable artificial intelligence: Foundations, applications and challenges* (pp. 245–61). IOS Press. https://doi.org/10.3233/SSW200022

Chari, S., Gruen, D. M., Seneviratne, O., & McGuinness, D. L. (2020b). Foundations of explainable knowledge-enabled systems. https://arxiv.org/abs/2003.07520

Cheyer, A., & Gruber, T. (2010). *Siri: A virtual personal assistant.* http://ontolog.cim3.net/file/resource/presentation/Siri_20100225/Siri--An-Ontology-driven-Application-for-the-Masses--AdamCheyer-TomGruber_20100225.pdf

Cheyer, A., & Guzzoni, D. (2006). *Method and apparatus for building an intelligent automated assistant* (US8677377B2). https://patents.google.com/patent/US8677377B2/en

Ching, A., Edunov, S., Kabiljo, M., Logothetis, D., & Muthukrishnan, S. (2015). One trillion edges: Graph processing at Facebook-scale. *Proceedings of the VLDB Endowment, 8*(12), 1804–15. https://doi.org/10.14778/2824032.2824077

Christophides, V., Efthymiou, V., & Stefanidis, K. (2015). *Entity resolution in the web of data.* Morgan & Claypool.

Coddington, M. A. (2019). *Aggregating the news: Secondhand knowledge and the erosion of journalistic authority.* Columbia University Press.

Coffa, J. A. (1991). *The semantic tradition from Kant to*

Carnap: To the Vienna station. Cambridge University Press.

Cohen, N. (2021, March 16). *Wikipedia is finally asking big tech to pay up.* Wired. https://www.wired.com/story /wikipedia-finally-asking-big-tech-to-pay-up

Columbia SPS. (2019a, June 10). *Deep learning for knowledge extraction and integration to build the Amazon Product Graph* [Video]. YouTube. https:// www.youtube.com/watch?v=focQXgMQ1gQ

Columbia SPS. (2019b, June 10). *Knowledge graphs in the enterprise: Lessons from customers of Amazon Neptune* [Video]. YouTube. https://www.youtube.com/watch?v= 3CdqXcnAeQQ

Cooke, R. (2021, January 14). *Wikipedia is the last best place on the internet.* Wired. https://www.wired .com/story/wikipedia-online-encyclopedia-best-place -internet/

Costanza-Chock, S. (2020). *Design justice: Community-led practices to build the worlds we need.* MIT Press.

Couldry, N., & Mejías, U. A. (2019). *The costs of connection: How data is colonizing human life and appropriating it for capitalism.* Stanford University Press.

Cui, S., & Shrouty, D. (2020, January 10). *Interest taxonomy: A knowledge graph management system for content understanding at Pinterest.* Pinterest Engingeering Blog. https://medium.com/pinterest -engineering/interest-taxonomy-a-knowledge-graph -management-system-for-content-understanding-at -pinterest-a6ae75c203fd

Curotto, P., & Hogan, A. (2020). Suggesting citations for Wikidata claims based on Wikipedia's external references. *1st Wikidata Workshop, 2020 International Semantic Web Conference.* https://wikidataworkshop .github.io/2020/papers/Wikidata_Workshop_2020 _paper_15.pdf

Dalvi, N., Kumar, R., Pang, B., Ramakrishnan, R., Tomkins, A., Bohannon, P., Keerthi, S., & Merugu, S.

(2009). A web of concepts. In *Proceedings of the twenty-eighth ACM SIGMOD-SIGACT-SIGART symposium on Principles of database systems (PODS '09)*. ACM. https://doi.org/10.1145/1559795.1559797

Davis, R., & Lenat, D. B. (1982). *Knowledge-based systems in artificial intelligence*. McGraw-Hill.

Day, R. E. (2000). The "conduit metaphor" and the nature and politics of information studies. *Journal of the American Society for Information Science, 51*(9), 805–11. https://doi.org/10.1002/(SICI)1097-4571(2000)51:9<805::AID-ASI30>3.0.CO;2-C

Day, R. E. (2001). *The modern invention of information: Discourse, history, and power*. Southern Illinois University Press.

de Saussure, F. (1916/2011). *Course in general linguistics*. Columbia University Press.

DeNardis, L. (2009). *Protocol politics: The globalization of internet governance*. MIT Press.

DeNardis, L. (2014). *The global war for internet governance*. MIT Press.

Dencik, L., Hintz, A., & Cable, J. (2016). Towards data justice? The ambiguity of anti-surveillance resistance in political activism. *Big Data & Society, 3*(2). https://doi.org/10.1177/2053951716679678

Devlin, J., Chang, M.-W., Lee, K., & Toutanova, K. (2019). BERT: Pre-training of deep bidirectional transformers for language understanding. In J. Burstein, C. Doran, & T. Solorio (Eds.), *Proceedings of the 2019 Conference of the North American Chapter of the Association for Computational Linguistics: Human language technologies, volume 1*. https://aclanthology.org/N19-1423/

Dewey, C. (2016, May 11). You probably haven't even noticed Google's sketchy quest to control the world's knowledge. *Washington Post*. https://www.washingtonpost.com/news/the-intersect/wp/2016/05/11/you-probably-havent-even-noticed-googles-sketchy-quest-to-control-the-worlds-knowledge/

Diakopoulos, N. (2019). *Automating the news: How algorithms are rewriting the media*. Harvard University Press.

Diaz, A. (2008). Through the Google goggles: Sociopolitical bias in search engine design. In A. Spink & M. Zimmer (Eds.), *Web search: Multidisciplinary perspectives* (pp. 11–34). Springer. https://doi.org/10.1007/978-3-540-75829-7_2

D'Ignazio, C., & Klein, L. F. (2020). *Data feminism*. MIT Press.

DiMaggio, P., Hargittai, E., Neuman, W. R., & Robinson, J. P. (2001). Social implications of the internet. *Annual Review of Sociology*, 27(1), 307–36. https://doi.org/10.1146/annurev.soc.27.1.307

Domingue, J., Fensel, D., & Hendler, J. A. (Eds.). (2011). *Handbook of semantic web technologies*. Springer.

Dong, H., Hussain, F. K., & Chang, E. (2008). A survey in semantic search technologies. *2nd IEEE International Conference on Digital Ecosystems and Technologies*, 403–8. https://doi.org/10.1109/DEST.2008.4635202

Dong, X., Gabrilovich, E., Heitz, G., Horn, W., Lao, N., Murphy, K., Strohmann, T., Sun, S., & Zhang, W. (2014). Knowledge vault: A web-scale approach to probabilistic knowledge fusion. In *Proceedings of the 20th ACM SIGKDD international conference on Knowledge discovery and data mining* (pp. 601–10). ACM. https://doi.org/10.1145/2623330.2623623

Dong, X. L., He, X., Kan, A., Li, X., Liang, Y., Ma, J., ... & Han, J. (2020). AutoKnow: Self-driving knowledge collection for products of thousands of types. In *Proceedings of the 26th ACM SIGKDD International Conference on Knowledge Discovery & Data Mining* (pp. 2724–34). ACM. https://doi.org/10.1145/3394486.3403323

Dourish, P. (2017). *The stuff of bits: An essay on the materialities of information*. MIT Press.

Duarte, M. E., & Belarde-Lewis, M. (2015). Imagining: Creating spaces for indigenous ontologies. *Cataloging and Classification Quarterly*, *53*(5–6), 677–702. https://doi.org/10.1080/01639374.2015.1018396

Dudfield, A., & Dodds, L. (2021). *Enriching ClaimReview for fact checkers*. Schema.org Blog. http://blog.schema.org/2021/12/enriching-claim-reviews-sharing.html

Dye, M., Ekanadham, C., Saluja, A., & Rastogi, A. (2020, December 10). *Supporting content decision makers with machine learning*. Netflix Technology Blog. https://netflixtechblog.com/supporting-content-decision-makers-with-machine-learning-995b7b76006f

Edwards, P. N., Bowker, G. C., Jackson, S. J., & Williams, R. (2009). Introduction: An agenda for infrastructure studies. *Journal of the Association for Information Systems*, *10*(5): 364–74. https://doi.org/10.17705/1jais.00200

Edwards, P. N., Jackson, S. J., Chalmers, M. K., Bowker, G. C., Borgman, C. L., Ribes, D., Burton, M. & Calvert, S. (2013) *Knowledge infrastructures: Intellectual frameworks and research challenges*. Deep Blue. http://knowledgeinfrastructures.org/

Elmer, G. (2003). *Profiling machines: Mapping the personal information economy*. MIT Press.

Erekhinskaya, T., Strebkov, D., Patel, S., Balakrishna, M., Tatu, M., & Moldovan, D. (2020, June). Ten ways of leveraging ontologies for natural language processing and its enterprise applications. In S. Groppe, L. Gruenwald, & V. Presutti (Eds.), *SBD '20: Proceedings of the International Workshop on Semantic Big Data* (pp. 1–6). ACM. https://doi.org/10.1145/3391274.3393639

Eriksson, M., Fleischer, R., Johansson, A., Snickars, P., & Vonderau, P. (2019). *Spotify teardown: Inside the black box of streaming music*. MIT Press.

Färber, M. (2019) The Microsoft Academic Knowledge Graph: A linked data source with 8 billion triples of scholarly data. In C. Ghidini, O. Hartig, M. Maleshkova, V. Svátek, I. Cruz, & A. Hogan (Eds.), *The Semantic*

Web – ISWC 2019. ISWC 2019. Springer. https://doi.org/10.1007/978-3-030-30796-7_8

Färber, M., Bartscherer, F., Menne, C., & Rettinger, A. (2018). Linked data quality of DBpedia, Freebase, OpenCyc, Wikidata, and YAGO. *Semantic Web Journal*, 9(1), 77–129. http://www.semantic-web-journal.net/system/files/swj1366.pdf

Färber, M., Ell, B., Menne, C., & Rettinger, A. (2015). A comparative survey of DBpedia, Freebase, OpenCyc, Wikidata, and YAGO. *Semantic Web Journal*, 1(1), 1–5. http://www.semantic-web-journal.net/system/files/swj1141.pdf

Feinberg, M. (2007). Hidden bias to responsible bias: An approach to information systems based on Haraway's situated knowledges. *Information Research*, 12(4), 12–14. http://informationr.net/ir/12-4/colis07.html

Feinberg, M. (2017). Reading databases: Slow information interactions beyond the retrieval paradigm. *Journal of Documentation*, 73(2), 336–56. https://doi.org/10.1108/JD-03-2016-0030

Fensel, D., Van Harmelen, F., Horrocks, I., McGuinness, D. L., & Patel-Schneider, P. F. (2001). OIL: An ontology infrastructure for the semantic web. *IEEE Intelligent Systems*, 16(2), 38–45. https://doi.org/10.1109/5254.920598

Ferguson, J. (2021, April 29). *SEO professionals: Stop sharing debunked zero-click search statistics.* Search Engine Journal. https://www.searchenginejournal.com/stop-quoting-zero-click-search-studies/403763/

Feuz, M., Fuller, M., & Stalder, F. (2011). Personal Web searching in the age of semantic capitalism: Diagnosing the mechanisms of personalisation. *First Monday*, 16(2). https://doi.org/10.5210/FM.V16I2.3344

Fidel, R. (2012). *Human information interaction: An ecological approach to information behavior.* MIT Press.

Fidler, B., & Acker, A. (2016). Metadata, infrastructure, and computer mediated communication in historical perspective. *Journal of the Association Information*

Science and Technology, 68(2), 412–22. https://doi.org/10.1002/asi.23660

Firth, J. R. (1957). *Papers in linguistics.* Oxford University Press.

Fishkin, R. (2019, August 13). *Less than half of Google searches now result in a click.* SparkToro. https://sparktoro.com/blog/less-than-half-of-google-searches-now-result-in-a-click/

Fishkin, R. (2021, March 22). *In 2020, two thirds of Google searches ended without a click.* SparkToro. https://sparktoro.com/blog/less-than-half-of-google-searches-now-result-in-a-click/

Floridi, L. (2011). *The philosophy of information.* Oxford University Press.

Floridi, L. (2018). Semantic capital: Its nature, value, and curation. *Philosophy & Technology, 31*(4), 481–97. https://doi.org/10.1007/s13347-018-0335-1

Ford, H. (2020). Rise of the underdog. In J. Reagle & J. Koerner (Eds.), *Wikipedia @ 20: Stories of an incomplete revolution* (pp. 189–201). MIT Press.

Ford, H. (2022). *Writing the revolution: Wikipedia and the survival of facts in the digital age.* MIT Press.

Ford, H., & Graham, M. (2016a). Provenance, power and place: Linked data and opaque digital geographies. *Environment and Planning D: Society and Space, 34*(6), 957–70. https://doi.org/10.1177/0263775816668857

Ford, H., & Graham, M. (2016b). Semantic cities: Coded geopolitics and the rise of the semantic web. In R. Kitchin & S.-Y. Perng (Eds.), *Code and the city* (pp. 200–14). Routledge.

Ford, H., & Vrandečić, D. (2020, December 10). *Automated facts, data contextualization and knowledge colonialism: A conversation between Denny Vrandečić and Heather Ford on Wikipedia's 20th Anniversary.* Big Data & Society Blog. https://bigdatasoc.blogspot.com/2020/12/automated-facts-data-contextualization.html

Fricker, M. (2007). *Epistemic injustice: Power and the ethics of knowing.* Oxford University Press.

Friedman, B., & Nissenbaum, H. (1996). Bias in computer systems. *ACM Transactions on Information Systems*, *14*(3), 330–47. https://doi.org/10.1145/230538.230561

Fuchs, C. (2009). Information and communication technologies and society: A contribution to the critique of the political economy of the internet. *European Journal of Communication*, *24*(1), 69–87. https://doi.org/10.1177/0267323108098947

Fürber, C. (2016). *Data quality management with semantic technologies*. Springer.

Gallagher, S. (2012, June 6). *How Google and Microsoft taught search to understand the web*. Ars Technica. https://arstechnica.com/information-technology/2012/06/inside-the-architecture-of-googles-knowledge-graph-and-microsofts-satori/

Gao, Y., Narayanan, A., Patterson, A., Taylor, J., & Jain, A. (2018, October 10). Panel: Enterprise-scale knowledge graphs. *17th International Semantic Web Conference (ISWC 2018)*. http://iswc2018.semanticweb.org/panel-enterprise-scale-knowledge-graphs/index.html

Garcez, A. A., & Lamb, L. C. (2020). Neurosymbolic AI: The 3rd wave. https://arxiv.org/abs/2012.05876

Gebru, T., Morgenstern, J., Vecchione, B., Vaughan, J. W., Wallach, H., Daumé III, H., & Crawford, K. (2021). Datasheets for datasets. *Communications of the ACM*, *64*(12), 86–92. https://doi.org/10.1145/3458723

Geeraerts, D. (2009). *Theories of lexical semantics*. Oxford University Press.

Gehl, R. (2014). *Reverse engineering social media: Software, culture, and political economy in new media capitalism*. Temple University Press.

Gerhart, S. L. (2004). Do Web search engines suppress controversy? *First Monday*, *9*(1). https://doi.org/10.5210/FM.V9I1.1111

Gerlitz, C., & Helmond, A. (2013). The like economy: Social buttons and the data-intensive web. *New Media & Society*, *15*(8), 1348–65. https://doi.org/10.1177/1461444812472322

Gillespie, T. (2010). The politics of "platforms." *New Media & Society*, *12*(3), 347–64. https://doi.org/10.1177/1461444809342738

Gillespie, T. (2018). *Custodians of the internet: Platforms, content moderation, and the hidden decisions that shape social media.* Yale University Press.

Ginsberg, A. (2008). Ontological indeterminacy and the semantic web. *International Journal on Semantic Web and Information Systems*, *4*(2), 19–48. https://doi.org/10.4018/JSWIS.2008040102

Glushko, R. J. (Ed.). (2013). *The discipline of organizing.* MIT Press.

Golden, P. (2019, September 5). *The tyranny of widgets: Schema.org and the enclosing of RDF* [Conference presentation]. Society for Social Studies of Science, New Orleans, USA. https://ptgolden.org/schema.pdf

Goldman, E. (2005). Search engine bias and the demise of search engine utopianism. *Yale Journal of Law & Technology*, *8*(1/6), 188–200.

Golumbia, D. (2009). *The cultural logic of computation.* Harvard University Press.

Gonçalves, R. S., Horridge, M., Li, R., Liu, Y., Musen, M. A., Nyulas, C. I., ... & Temple, D. (2019, October). Use of OWL and Semantic Web technologies at Pinterest. In C. Ghidini, O. Hartig, M. Maleshkova, V. Svátek, I. Cruz, A. Hogan, J. Song, M. Lefrançois, & F. Gandon (Eds.), *The Semantic Web – ISWC 2019* (pp. 418–35). Springer.

Google. (2019, February 16). *How Google fights disinformation.* Google Blog. https://www.blog.google/documents/37/How_Google_Fights_Disinformation.pdf

Google Search Central. (2020, January 31). *English Google Webmaster Central office-hours from January 31, 2020* [Video]. YouTube. https://www.youtube.com/watch?v=ylRoKGSSqd8

Graham, M. (2015, November 30). *Why does Google say Jerusalem is the capital of Israel?* Slate. https://slate.com

/technology/2015/11/why-does-google-say-jerusalem-is-the-capital-of-israel.html

Graham, M., & Sengupta, A. (2017, October 5). *We're all connected now, so why is the internet so white and western? The Guardian.* https://www.theguardian.com/commentisfree/2017/oct/05/internet-white-western-google-wikipedia-skewed

Graham, R. (2014). A "history" of search engines: Mapping technologies of memory, learning and discovery. In R. König & M. Rasch (Eds.), *Society of the query reader: Reflections on web search* (pp. 105–20). Institute of Network Cultures.

Granka, L. A. (2010). The politics of search: A decade retrospective. *The Information Society,* 26(5), 364–73. https://doi.org/10.1080/01972243.2010.511560

Graves, M., Constabaris, A., & Brickley, D. (2007). FOAF: Connecting people on the semantic web. *Cataloging & Classification Quarterly,* 43(3–4), 191–202. https://doi.org/10.1300/J104v43n03_10

Gray, J., Gerlitz, C., & Bounegru, L. (2018). Data infrastructure literacy. *Big Data & Society,* 5(2), 1–13. https://doi.org/10.1177/2053951718786316

Grimmelmann, J. (2007). The structure of search engine law. *Iowa Law Review,* 93(1), 1–63. https://scholarship.law.cornell.edu/facpub/1547/

Grimmelmann, J. (2009). The Google dilemma. *New York Law School Law Review,* 53(4), 939–50. https://digitalcommons.nyls.edu/nyls_law_review/vol53/iss4/12/

Grimmelmann, J. (2014). Speech engines. *Minnesota Law Review,* 98(3), 868–952. https://minnesotalawreview.org/article/speech-engines/

Grind, K., Schechner, S., McMillan, R., & West, J. (2019, November 15). How Google interferes with its search algorithms and changes your results. *Wall Street Journal.* https://www.wsj.com/articles/how-google-interferes-with-its-search-algorithms-and-changes-your-results-11573823753

Gruber, T. R. (1991). The role of common ontology in achieving sharable, reusable knowledge bases. In J. A. Allen, R. Fikes, & E. Sandewall (Eds.), *Principles of knowledge representation and reasoning: Proceedings of the second international conference* (pp. 601–2).

Gruber, T. R. (1993a). A translation approach to portable ontology specifications. *Knowledge Acquisition*, 5(2), 199–220. https://doi.org/10.1006/knac.1993.1008

Gruber, T. R. (1993b). Toward principles for the design of ontologies used for knowledge sharing. In N. Guarino & R. Poli (Eds.), *International workshop on formal ontology*. Kluwer Academic.

Gruber, T. R. (1995). Toward principles for the design of ontologies used for knowledge sharing. *International Journal of Human-Computer Studies*, 43(5–6), 907–28.

Gruber, T. R. (2009a). Ontology. In L. Liu & M. T. Özsu (Eds.), *Encyclopedia of database systems*. Springer.

Gruber, T. R. (2009b). *Siri: A virtual personal assistant*. https://tomgruber.org/writing/Siri-SemTech09.pdf

Gruber, T. R., Cheyer, A. J., Kittlaus, D., Guzzoni, D. R., Brigham, C. D., Giuli, R. D., Bastea-Forte, M., & Saddler, H. J. (2010). *Intelligent automated assistant* (US20120016678A1). https://patents.google.com/patent/US20120016678A1/en

Guarino, N., Oberle, D., & Staab, S. (2009). What is an ontology? In S. Staab & R. Studer (Eds.), *Handbook on ontologies* (pp. 1–17). Springer.

Gubin, M., Sung, S., Bharat, K., & Dauber, K. W. (2014). *Entity identification model training* (US9251141B1). https://patents.google.com/patent/US9251141B1/

Guha, R. V. (1992). *Contexts: A formalization and some applications* [Doctoral dissertation, Stanford University].

Guha, R. V., & Bray, T. (1997, June 6). *Meta content framework using XML*. W3C. https://www.w3.org/TR/NOTE-MCF-XML/

Guha, R. V., Brickley, D., & MacBeth, S. (2016). Schema. org: Evolution of structured data on the Web: Big data makes common schemas even more necessary.

Queue, 13(9), 10–37. https://doi.org/10.1145/2857274 .2857276

Guha, R. V., McCool, R., & Miller, E. (2003). Semantic search. *Proceedings of the 12th International Conference on World Wide Web, WWW 2003* (pp. 700–9). https://doi.org/10.1145/775152.775250

Guns, R. (2013). Tracing the origins of the semantic web. *Journal of the American Society for Information Science and Technology, 64*(10), 2173–81. https://doi.org/10 .1002/ASI.22907

Gupta, R., Sun, S., Blitzer, J., Lin, D., & Gabrilovich, E. (2014). *Question answering to populate knowledge base* (US10108700B2). https://patents.google.com /patent/US10108700B2/

Gutiérrez, C., & Sequeda, J. F. (2020). Knowledge graphs: A tutorial on the history of knowledge graph's main ideas. *CIKM '20: Proceedings of the 29th ACM International Conference on Information and Knowledge Management* (pp. 3509–10). https://doi.org /10.1145/3340531.3412176

Gutiérrez, C., & Sequeda, J. F. (2021). Knowledge graphs. *Communications of the ACM, 64*(3), 96–104. https://dl .acm.org/doi/10.1145/3418294

Guzman, A. L. (2017). Making AI safe for humans: A conversation with Siri. In R. W. Gehl & M. Bakardjieva (Eds.), *Socialbots and their friends: Digital media and the automation of sociality*. Routledge.

Guzman, A. L. (Ed.). (2018). *Human-machine communication: Rethinking communication, technology, and ourselves*. Peter Lang.

Haider, J., & Sundin, O. (2019). *Invisible search and online search engines: The ubiquity of search in everyday life*. Routledge.

Halavais, A. (2008/2017). *Search engine society* (2nd ed.). Polity.

Halevy, A., Norvig, P., & Pereira, F. (2009). The unreasonable effectiveness of data. *IEEE Intelligent Systems, 24*(2), 8–12.

Halford, S., Pope, C., & Weal, M. (2013). Digital futures? Sociological challenges and opportunities in the emergent semantic web. *Sociology, 47*(1), 173–89. https://doi.org/10.1177/0038038512453798

Halpin, H. (2013). *Social semantics: The search for meaning on the Web.* Springer.

Halpin, H., Hayes, P. J., McCusker, J. P., McGuinness, D. L., & Thompson, H. S. (2010). When owl:sameAs isn't the same: An analysis of identity in linked data. *The Semantic Web – ISWC 2010. Lecture Notes in Computer Science, vol. 6496* (pp. 305–20). Springer. https://doi.org/10.1007/978-3-642-17746-0_20

Halpin, H., & Monnin, A. (Eds.). (2014). *Philosophical engineering: Toward a philosophy of the Web.* Wiley Blackwell.

Hargittai, E. (2007). The social, political, economic and cultural dimensions of search engines: An introduction. *Journal of Computer-Mediated Communication, 12*(3), 769–77. https://doi.org/10.1111/j.1083-6101.2007.00349.x

Hartig, O. (2009). Provenance information in the web of data. *Proceedings of the Linked Data on the Web Workshop (LDOW '09), Madrid, Spain.* http://events.linkeddata.org/ldow2009/papers/ldow2009_paper18.pdf

Harzing, A.-W. (2018, November 24). *Google Scholar profiles: The good, the bad, and the better.* https://harzing.com/blog/2018/11/google-scholar-citation-profiles-the-good-the-bad-and-the-better

Haugen, A. (2010). Abstract: The Open Graph Protocol design decisions. In *Proceedings of the 9th international semantic web conference (ISWC '10)* (p. 338). Springer. https://link.springer.com/chapter/10.1007/978-3-642-17749-1_25

Hayes, P. J., & Halpin, H. (2008). In defense of ambiguity. *International Journal on Semantic Web and Information Systems, 4*(2), 1–18. https://doi.org/10.4018/jswis.2008040101

Hayes-Roth, F., Waterman, D. A., & Lenat, D. B. (1983). *Building expert systems*. Addison-Wesley.

Heist, N., Hertling, S., Ringler, D., & Paulheim, H. (2020). Knowledge graphs on the web: An overview. https://arxiv.org/abs/2003.00719

Helmond, A. (2015). The platformization of the web: Making web data platform ready. *Social Media + Society*, 1(2), 1–11. https://doi.org/10.1177/2056305115603080

Hendler, J., & McGuinness, D. L. (2000). The DARPA agent markup language. *IEEE Intelligent systems*, 15(6), 67–73.

Henry, J. W. (2012). *Providing knowledge panels with search results* (US9268820B2). https://patents.google.com/patent/US9268820B2/en

Hernández, I., Gupta, P., Rosso, P., & Rocha, M. (2012). A simple model for classifying web queries by user intent. In *Proc. 2nd Spanish Conf. on information retrieval* (pp. 235–40).

Hillis, K., Petit, M., & Jarrett, K. (2012). *Google and the culture of search*. Routledge.

Hitzler, P. (2021). A review of the semantic web field. *Communications of the ACM*, 64(2), 76–83.

Hoffmann, A. L. (2019). Where fairness fails: Data, algorithms, and the limits of antidiscrimination discourse. *Information, Communication & Society*, 22(7), 900–15. https://doi.org/10.1080/1369118X.2019.1573912

Hogan, A. (2020). *The web of data*. Springer.

Hogan, A., Blomqvist, E., Cochez, M., D'Amato, C., de Melo, G., Gutiérrez, C., … Zimmermann, A. (2021). Knowledge graphs. *ACM Computing Surveys*, 54(4), 1–37. https://doi.org/10.1145/3447772

Hogenhout, L. (2021). A framework for ethical AI at the United Nations. https://arxiv.org/abs/2104.12547

Hogue, A. W., & Betz, J. T. (2006). *Browseable fact repository* (US20070198503A1). https://patents.google.com/patent/US20070198503A1/en

Houser, N. (1992). The scope of Peirce's semiotics. In M. Balat & J. Deledalle-Rhodes (Eds.), *Signs of*

Humanity/L'homme et ses signes, vol. III (pp. 1283–9). Mouton de Gruyter.

Hu, Y. (2005). Efficient, high-quality force-directed graph drawing. *Mathematica Journal, 10*(1), 37–71.

Huang, P. S., Zhang, H., Jiang, R., Stanforth, R., Welbl, J., Rae, J., … & Kohli, P. (2019). Reducing sentiment bias in language models via counterfactual evaluation. https://arxiv.org/abs/1911.03064

Hui, Y. (2016). *On the existence of digital objects.* University of Minnesota Press.

Iliadis, A. (2018). Algorithms, ontology, and social progress. *Global Media and Communication, 14*(2), 219–30. https://doi.org/10.1177/1742766518776688

Iliadis, A. (2019). The Tower of Babel problem: Making data make sense with Basic Formal Ontology. *Online Information Review, 43*(6), 1021–45. https://doi.org/10.1108/OIR-07-2018-0210

Iliadis, A. (2020). Computer guts and swallowed sensors: Ingestibles made palatable in an era of embodied computing. In I. Pedersen & A. Iliadis (Eds.), *Embodied computing: Wearables, implantables, embeddables, ingestibles* (pp. 1–20). MIT Press.

Iliadis, A. (2022). Critical and cultural approaches to human-machine communication. In A. L. Guzman, R. McEwen, & S. Jones (Eds.), *The SAGE handbook of human-machine communication.* Sage.

Iliadis, A., & Acker, A. (2022). The seer and the seen: Surveying Palantir's surveillance platform. *The Information Society, 38*(5). https://doi.org/10.1080/01972243.2022.2100851

Iliadis, A., Liao, T., Pedersen, I., & Han, J. (2021). Learning about metadata and machines: Teaching students using a novel structured database activity. *Journal of Communication Pedagogy, 4,* 152–65. https://doi.org/10.31446/JCP.2021.1.14

Iliadis, A., & Pedersen, I. (2018). The fabric of digital life: Uncovering sociotechnical tradeoffs in embodied computing through metadata. *Journal of Information,*

Communication and Ethics in Society, *16*(3), 311–27. https://doi.org/10.1108/jices-03-2018-0022

Iliadis, A., & Russo, F. (2016). Critical data studies: An introduction. *Data & Society*, *3*(2), 1–7. https://doi.org /10.1177/2053951716674238

Ilievski, F., Szekely, P., & Schwabe, D. (2020). Commonsense knowledge in Wikidata. https://arxiv .org/abs/2008.08114

Ingraham, N. (2012, May 17). Google calls Knowledge Graph first baby step towards "Star Trek computer." *Washington Post*. https://www.washingtonpost.com /business/technology/google-engineer-calls-knowledge -graph-first-baby-step-towards-star-trek-computer /2012/05/17/gIQAoGdhVU_story.html

Innis, H. A. (1951). *The bias of communication*. University of Toronto Press.

Introna, L. & Nissenbaum, H. (2000). Shaping the web: Why the politics of search engines matters. *The Information Society*, *16*(3), 1–17. https://doi.org/10 .1080/01972240050133634

Jacoby, S. (2016, October 7). In the Google age, knowledge (without clicking) still matters. *Washington Post*. https:// www.washingtonpost.com/opinions/in-the-google-age -knowledge-without-clicking-still-matters/2016/10/05 /8ad8eb9a-7e87-11e6-8d0c-fb6c00c90481_story.html

Jacomy, M., Venturini, T., Heymann, S., & Bastian, M. (2014). ForceAtlas2, a continuous graph layout algorithm for handy network visualization designed for the Gephi software. *PLoS ONE*, *9*(6), e98679. https:// doi.org/10.1371/journal.pone.0098679

Jeanneney, J.-N. (2006). *Google and the myth of universal knowledge: A view from Europe*. University of Chicago Press.

Jeffries, A. (2020, October 20). *In historic antitrust lawsuit, DOJ cites banned words and Google self-preferencing as supporting evidence*. The Markup. https://themarkup .org/google-the-giant/2020/10/20/google-antitrust -lawsuit-markup-investigations

Jeffries, A., & Yin, L. (2020, July 28). *Google's top search result? Surprise! It's Google.* The Markup. https://themarkup.org/google-the-giant/2020/07/28 /google-search-results-prioritize-google-products-over -competitors

Jenkins, H. (2004). The cultural logic of media convergence. *International Journal of Cultural Studies*, 7(1), 33–43. https://doi.org/10.1177/1367877904040603

Ji, L., Wang, Y., Shi, B., Zhang, D., Wang, Z., & Yan, J. (2019). Microsoft Concept Graph: Mining semantic concepts for short text understanding. *Data Intelligence*, 1(3), 238–70. https://doi.org/10.1162/dint_a_00013

Joudrey, D. N., & Taylor, A. G. (2018). *The organization of information.* Libraries Unlimited.

Kaldrack, I., & Röhle, T. (2014). Divide and share: Taxonomies, orders and masses in Facebook's Open Graph. *Computational Culture*, 4. http:// computationalculture.net/divide-and-share

Karasti, H., Millerand, F., Hine, C. M., & Bowker, G. C. (2016). Knowledge infrastructures. *Science & Technology Studies*, 29(1), 2–12.

Karppi, T. (2018). *Disconnect: Facebook's affective bonds.* University of Minnesota Press.

Kasenchak, B. (2019). *What is semantic search? And why is it important?* Discover and Online Search, Part Two: Personalized Content, Personal Data (Webinar). https:// www.slideshare.net/BaltimoreNISO/kasenchak-what-is -semantic-search-and-why-is-it-important

Kejriwal, M., Knoblock, C., & Szekely, P. (2021). *Knowledge graphs: Fundamentals, techniques, and applications.* MIT Press.

Kejriwal, M., & Szekely, P. (2017) An investigative search engine for the human trafficking domain. In C. d'Amato et al. (Eds.), *The Semantic Web – ISWC 2017. Lecture notes in computer science, vol. 10588* (pp. 247–62). Springer. https://doi.org/10.1007/978-3-319-68204 -4_25

Kelley, L. (2019, September 23). *The Google feature*

magnifying disinformation. The Atlantic. https://www
.theatlantic.com/technology/archive/2019/09/googles
-knowledge-panels-are-magnifying-disinformation
/598474/

Kendall, E. F., & McGuinness, D. L. (2019). *Ontology engineering*. Morgan & Claypool.

Klinger, U., & Svensson, J. (2015). The emergence of network media logic in political communication: A theoretical approach. *New Media & Society*, *17*(8), 1241–57. https://doi.org/10.1177/1461444814522952

Knorr Cetina, K. (1999). *Epistemic cultures: How the sciences make knowledge*. Harvard University Press.

Knublauch, H., & Kontokostas, D. (2017). *Shapes Constraint Language (SHACL)*. W3C. https://www.w3
.org/TR/shacl/

Koerner, J. (2020). Wikipedia has a bias problem. In J. Reagle & J. Koerner (Eds.), *Wikipedia @ 20: Stories of an incomplete revolution* (pp. 311–21). MIT Press.

Kofler, C., Larson, M., & Hanjalic, A. (2016). User intent in multimedia search: A survey of the state of the art and future challenges. *ACM Computing Surveys*, *49*(2), 1–37. https://doi.org/10.1145/2954930

Kolbe, A. (2015, December 2). *Whither Wikidata?* The Signpost. https://en.wikipedia.org/wiki/Wikipedia:
Wikipedia_Signpost/2015-12-02/Op-ed

Kollar, T., Berry, D., Stuart, L., Owczarzak, K., Chung, T., Mathias, L., … & Matsoukas, S. (2018). The Alexa meaning representation language. In S. Bangalore, J. Chu-Carroll, & Y. Li (Eds.), *Proceedings of the 2018 conference of the North American Chapter of the Association for Computational Linguistics: Human language technologies, Volume 3* (pp. 177–84). ACL.

König, R., & Rasch, M. (Eds.). (2014). *Society of the query reader: Reflections on web search*. Institute of Network Cultures.

Kostopoulos, T. (2022). Cleansing Greece of the miasma of its "Sudeten": The Macedonian Slavs as an unwanted minority in the aftermath of World War II. In O. Konrád,

B. Barth, & J. Mrňka (Eds.), *Collective identities and post-war violence in Europe, 1944–48* (pp. 91–127). Palgrave Macmillan.

Krämer, B., & Conrad, J. (2017). Social ontologies online: The representation of social structures on the internet: *Social Media + Society, 3*(1). https://doi.org/10.1177/2056305117693648

Kremers, H. (Ed.). (2020). *Digital cultural heritage.* Springer.

Langlois, G. (2014). *Meaning in the age of social media.* Palgrave Macmillan.

Lassila, O., & Swick, R. R. (1999, January 5). *Resource description framework (RDF) model and syntax specification.* W3C. https://www.w3.org/TR/PR-rdf-syntax/Overview.html

Leazer, G. H., & Montoya, R. (2020). The politics of knowledge organization: Introduction to the special issue. *Knowledge Organization, 47*(5), 367–71.

Lenat, D. B. (1989). Ontological versus knowledge engineering. *IEEE Transactions on Knowledge and Data Engineering, 1*(1), 84–8. https://doi.org/10.1109/69.43405

Lenat, D. B. (1995). Cyc: A large-scale investment in knowledge infrastructure. *Communications of the ACM, 38*(11), 33–8. https://doi.org/10.1145/219717.219745

Lenat, D. B., & Guha, R. V. (1989). *Building large knowledge-based systems; Representation and inference in the Cyc project.* Addison-Wesley.

Lenat, D. B., Guha, R. V., Pittman, K., Pratt, D., & Shepherd, M. (1990). Cyc: Toward programs with common sense. *Communications of the ACM, 33*(8), 30–49. https://doi.org/10.1145/79173.79176

Lenat, D. B., Prakash, M., & Shepherd, M. (1985). CYC: Using common sense knowledge to overcome brittleness and knowledge acquisition bottlenecks. *AI Magazine, 6*(4), 65. https://doi.org/10.1609/aimag.v6i4.510

Lewis, M., Liu, Y., Goyal, N., Ghazvininejad, M., Mohamed, A., Levy, O., Stoyanov, V., & Zettlemoyer,

L. (2020). BART: Denoising sequence-to-sequence pre-training for natural language generation, translation, and comprehension. arXiv:1910.13461

Li, E. (2019, August 16). *Pin2Interest: A scalable system for content classification.* Pinterest Engineering Blog. https://medium.com/pinterest-engineering /pin2interest-a-scalable-system-for-content -classification-41a586675ee7

Liao, T., & Iliadis, A. (2021). A future so close: Mapping 10 years of promises and futures across the augmented reality development cycle. *New Media & Society, 23*(2), 258–83. https://doi.org/10.1177/1461444820924623

Lih, A. (2009). *The Wikipedia revolution: How a bunch of nobodies created the world's greatest encyclopedia.* Hachette Books.

Lim, S. (2019, April 18). *A better ClaimReview to grow a global fact-check database.* Duke Reporters' Lab. https://reporterslab.org/a-better-claimreview-to-grow -a-global-fact-check-database/

Lim, Y. J., Linn, J., Liang, Y., Steinebach, C., Lu, W. L., Kim, D. H. ... Yang, M. (2017). *Predicting intent of a search for a particular context* (WO2018213326A1). https:// patents.google.com/patent/WO2018213326A1/en

Lin, T., Pantel, P., Gamon, M., Kannan, A., & Fuxman, A. (2012, April). Active objects: Actions for entity-centric search. In *Proceedings of the 21st international conference on World Wide Web* (pp. 589–98). https:// doi.org/10.1145/2187836.2187916

Lindenberg, F. (2020a, August 11). *Here's why investigative reporters need to know knowledge graphs.* Global Investigative Journalism Network. https://gijn .org/2020/08/11/heres-why-investigative-reporters-need -to-know-knowledge-graphs/

Lindenberg, F. (2020b, July 11). *Things, not strings: Knowledge graphs for investigative reporting.* OCCRP: Unreported. https://medium.com/occrp-unreported /things-not-strings-knowledge-graphs-for-investigative -reporting-9d8a26913f65

Littletree, S., Belarde-Lewis, M., & Duarte, M. (2020). Centering relationality: A conceptual model to advance indigenous knowledge organization practices. *Knowledge Organization*, 47(5), 410–26. https://www.ergon-verlag .de/isko_ko/downloads/ko_47_2020_5_e.pdf

Liu, D., Mikroyannidi, E., & Lee, R. (2014). Semantic web technologies supporting the BBC knowledge & learning beta online pages. In *LILE @ ISWC*. http://ceur -ws.org/Vol-1254/1_liu.pdf

Loukissas, Y. A. (2019). *All data are local: Thinking critically in a data-driven society*. MIT Press.

Mackenzie, A. (2017). *Machine learners: Archaeology of a data practice*. MIT Press.

Mager, A. (2012). Algorithmic ideology: How capitalist society shapes search engines. *Information, Communication & Society*, 15(5), 769–87. https://doi .org/10.1080/1369118X.2012.676056

Mannes, J. (2016, November 2). *Microsoft strives to give computers common sense with Concept Graph*. TechCrunch. https://techcrunch.com/2016/11/01 /microsoft-strives-to-give-computers-common-sense -with-concept-graph/

Mantzarlis, A. (2019, Decemeber 19). *How we highlight fact checks in Search and Google News*. Google Blog. https://blog.google/outreach-initiatives/google-news -initiative/how-we-highlight-fact-checks-search-and -google-news/

Markoff, J. (2007, March 9). *Start-up aims for database to automate web searching. The New York Times*. https://www.nytimes.com/2007/03/09/technology /09data.html

Markoff, J. (2008, December 14). *A software secretary that takes charge. The New York Times*. https://www .nytimes.com/2008/12/14/business/14stream.html ?_r=1

Matei, S. A., & Britt, B. C. (2017). *Structural differentiation in social media: Adhocracy, entropy, and the "1% effect"*. Springer.

Matei, S. A., & Dobrescu, C. (2011). Wikipedia's "neutral point of view:" Settling conflict through ambiguity. *The Information Society*, 27(1), 1–12. https://doi.org /10.1080/01972243.2011.534368

Mayernik, M. S., & Acker, A. (2018). Tracing the traces: The critical role of metadata within networked communications. *Journal of the Association for Information Science and Technology*, 69(1), 177–80. https://doi.org /10.1002/asi.23927

McCarthy, J. (1958). Programs with common sense. *Proceedings of the Symposium on the Mechanization of Thought Processes*. HMSO.

McCarthy, M. T. (2017). The semantic web and its entanglements. *Science, Technology and Society*, 22(1), 21–37. https://doi.org/10.1177/0971721816682796

McChesney, R. W. (2013). *Digital disconnect: How capitalism is turning the internet against democracy*. The New Press.

McComb, D. (2004). *Semantics in business systems: The savvy manager's guide*. Morgan Kaufmann.

McComb, D. (2018). *Software wasteland: How the application-centric mindset is hobbling our enterprises*. Technics Publications.

McDowell, Z. J., & Vetter, M. A. (2021). *Wikipedia and the representation of reality*. Routledge.

McGuinness, D. L., & van Harmelen, F. (2004, February 10). *OWL web ontology language overview*. W3C. https://www.w3.org/TR/owl-features/

McMahon, C., Johnson, I., & Hecht, B. (2017, May). The substantial interdependence of Wikipedia and Google: A case study on the relationship between peer production communities and information technologies. *Proceedings of the 11th International Conference on Web and Social Media, ICWSM 2017* (pp. 142–51).

Menzel, J. (2010, July 16). *Deeper understanding with Metaweb*. Google Blog. https://googleblog.blogspot .com/2010/07/deeper-understanding-with-metaweb .html

Metz, C. (2016, March 24). *One genius' lonely crusade to teach a computer common sense*. Wired. https://www.wired.com/2016/03/doug-lenat-artificial-intelligence-common-sense-engine/

Metzler, D., Tay, Y., Bahri, D., & Najork, M. (2021). Rethinking search: Making domain experts out of dilettantes. *ACM SIGIR Forum*, *55*(1), 1–27. https://doi.org/10.1145/3476415.3476428

Mikolov, T., Chen, K., Corrado, G., & Dean, J. (2013). Efficient estimation of word representations in vector space. https://arxiv.org/abs/1301.3781

Mikroyannidi, E., Liu D., & Lee R. (2016) Use of semantic web technologies in the architecture of the BBC education online pages. In D. Mouromtsev & M. d'Aquin (Eds.), *Open data for education. Lecture notes in computer science, vol. 9500*. Springer. https://doi.org/10.1007/978-3-319-30493-9_4

Miller, G. A. (1995). WordNet: a lexical database for English. *Communications of the ACM*, *38*(11), 39–41. https://doi.org/10.1145/219717.219748

Miller, G. A., Beckwith, R., Fellbaum, C., Gross, D., & Miller, K. J. (1990). Introduction to WordNet: An on-line lexical database. *International Journal of Lexicography*, *3*(4), 235–44. https://doi.org/10.1093/ijl/3.4.235

Monea, A. (2016). The graphing of difference: Numerical mediation and the case of Google's Knowledge Graph. *Cultural Studies ↔ Critical Methodologies*, *16*(5), 452–61. https://doi.org/10.1177/1532708616655763

Mosco, V. (1996/2009). *The political economy of communication* (2nd ed.). Sage.

Mulvin, D. (2021). *Proxies: The cultural work of standing in*. MIT Press.

Nadeem, M., Bethke, A., & Reddy, S. (2020). Stereoset: Measuring stereotypical bias in pretrained language models. https://arxiv.org/abs/2004.09456

Napoli, P. N., & Caplan, R. (2017). Why media companies insist they're not media companies, why they're wrong, and why it matters. *First Monday*, 22(5). https://doi.org /10.5210/fm.v22i5.7051

Nayak, P. (2020, September 10). *Our latest investments in information quality in Search and News*. Google Blog. https://blog.google/products/search/our-latest -investments-information-quality-search-and-news

Ni, C. C., Sum Liu, K., & Torzec, N. (2020, April). Layered graph embedding for entity recommendation using Wikipedia in the Yahoo! Knowledge Graph. In A. E. F. Seghrouchni, G. Sukthankar, T-Y. Liu, & M. van Steen (Eds.), *WWW '20: Companion proceedings of the web conference 2020* (pp. 811–18). https://doi.org/10 .1145/3366424.3383570

Noble, S. U. (2018). *Algorithms of oppression: How search engines reinforce racism*. New York University Press.

Noy, N., Burgess, M., & Brickley, D. (2019a). Google Dataset Search: Building a search engine for datasets in an open Web ecosystem. In L. Liu & R. White (Eds.), *Proceedings of the 2019 World Wide Web Conference (WWW '19), May 13–17, 2019, San Francisco, CA, USA*. ACM. https://doi.org/10.1145/3308558.3313685

Noy, N., Gao, Y., Jain, A., Patterson, A., Narayanan, A., & Taylor, J. (2019b). Industry-scale Knowledge Graphs: Lessons and challenges. *Queue*, 17(2), 48–75. https://doi.org/10.1145/3329781.3332266

Noy, N., Gao, Y., Jain, A., Patterson, A., Narayanan, A., & Taylor, J. (2019c). Industry-scale knowledge graphs. *Communications of the ACM*, 62(8), 36–43. https://doi .org/10.1145/3331166

Obrst, L. (2003). Ontologies for semantically inter-operable systems. In *CIKM '03: Proceedings of the twelfth international conference on Information and knowledge management* (pp. 366–9). https://doi.org/10 .1145/956863.956932

Ogbuji, U. (2017, December 5). *Introduction to the Schema.org information model*. IBM Developer. https:// developer.ibm.com/series/schemaorg/

Ojeda, C. (2019). The political responses of virtual assistants. *Social Science Computer Review*, *39*(5), 884–902. https://doi.org/10.1177/0894439319886844

Olanoff, D., Constine, J., Taylor, C., & Lunden, I. (2013, January 15). *Facebook announces its third pillar "Graph Search" that gives you answers, not links like Google*. TechCrunch. https://techcrunch.com/2013/01/15/facebook-announces-its-third-pillar-graph-search/

Olson, H. A. (2001). The power to name: Representation in library catalogs. *Signs: Journal of Women in Culture and Society*, *26*(3), 639–68. https://doi.org/10.1086/495624

Olson, H. A. (2002). *The power to name: Locating the limits of subject representation in libraries*. Springer.

Owen, L. H. (2019, March 25). *The long, complicated, and extremely frustrating history of Medium, 2012–present*. NiemanLab. https://www.niemanlab.org/2019/03/the-long-complicated-and-extremely-frustrating-history-of-medium-2012-present/

Pablo, C. de. (2020, July 16). *How Wikidata might help the Smithsonian with its mission to diffuse knowledge*. https://wikiedu.org/blog/2020/07/16/how-wikidata-might-help-the-smithsonian-with-its-mission-to-diffuse-knowledge/

Paris, B. S. (2021). Time constructs: Design ideology and a future internet. *Time & Society*, *30*(1), 126–49. https://doi.org/10.1177/0961463X20985316

Parker, J. (2017). *Siri says the national anthem of Bulgaria is 'Despacito.'* CNET. https://www.cnet.com/tech/mobile/icymi-the-national-anthem-of-bulgaria-is-despacito/

Patel-Schneider, P.F. (2014). Analyzing Schema.org. In P. Mika et al. (Eds.), *The Semantic Web – ISWC 2014. Lecture Notes in Computer Science, vol. 8796* (pp. 261–76). Springer. https://doi.org/10.1007/978-3-319-11964-9_17

Pedersen, I., & Iliadis, A. (Eds.). (2020). *Embodied computing: Wearables, implantables, embeddables, ingestibles*. MIT Press.

Peirce, C. S. (1894/1998). What is a sign? In N. Houser & the Peirce Edition Project (Eds.), *The Essential Peirce, Volume 2: Selected Philosophical Writings, 1893–1913* (pp. 4–10). Indiana University Press.

Peirce, C. S. (1895/1998). Of reasoning in general. In N. Houser & the Peirce Edition Project (Eds.), *The Essential Peirce, Volume 2: Selected Philosophical Writings, 1893–1913* (pp. 11–26). Indiana University Press.

Perera, V., Chung, T., Kollar, T., & Strubell, E. (2018). Multi-task learning for parsing the Alexa meaning representation language. *Proceedings of the AAAI Conference on Artificial Intelligence*, 32(1), 5390–7. https://ojs.aaai.org/index.php/AAAI/article/view/12019

Pérez, S. (2012, March 30). *Wikipedia's next big thing: Wikidata, a machine-readable, user-editable database funded by Google, Paul Allen and others*. TechCrunch. https://techcrunch.com/2012/03/30/wikipedias-next -big-thing-wikidata-a-machine-readable-user-editable -database-funded-by-google-paul-allen-and-others/

Pew Research Center (2017, December 12). *Nearly half of Americans use digital voice assistants, mostly on their smartphones.* https://www.pewresearch.org/fact-tank /2017/12/12/nearly-half-of-americans-use-digital-voice -assistants-mostly-on-their-smartphones/

Pew Research Center (2021, January 12). *News use across social media platforms in 2020*. https://www .pewresearch.org/journalism/2021/01/12/news-use -across-social-media-platforms-in-2020/

Plantin, J. C., Lagoze, C., & Edwards, P. N. (2018a). Re-integrating scholarly infrastructure: The ambiguous role of data sharing platforms. *Big Data & Society*, 5(1). https://doi.org/10.1177/2053951718756683

Plantin, J.-C., Lagoze, C., Edwards, P. N., & Sandvig, C. (2018b). Infrastructure studies meet platform studies in the age of Google and Facebook. *New Media & Society*, 20(1), 293–310. https://doi.org/10.1177 /1461444816661553

Pogue, D. (2012, May 23). *Going beyond search, into*

fetch. The New York Times. https://www.nytimes .com/2012/05/24/technology/personaltech/google-and -microsoft-feature-do-it-all-search-pages-state-of-the -art.html

Poirier, L. (2019). Classification as catachresis: Double binds of representing difference with semiotic infra-structure. *Canadian Journal of Communication, 44*(3). https://doi.org/10.22230/cjc.2019v44n3a3455

Pomerantz, J. (2015). *Metadata.* MIT Press.

Poovey, M. (1998). *A history of the modern fact: Problems of knowledge in the sciences of wealth and society.* University of Chicago Press.

Postigo, H. (2021). Hacking diversity into creative artificial intelligence-assessment: Categorization and remedies for gender and race bias in natural language processing models for the creative industries. *AoIR selected papers of internet research proceedings.* Virtual Event. AoIR. https://spir.aoir.org/ojs/index.php/spir/article/view /12131/10500

Poulter, M., & Ahmed, W. (2021). Representation of non-western cultural knowledge on Wikipedia: The case of the visual arts. https://www.preprints.org/manuscript /202104.0770/v1

Prud'hommeaux, E., & Seaborne, A. (2008). *SPARQL Query Language for RDF.* W3C. https://www.w3.org /TR/rdf-sparql-query/

Qian, R. (2013, March 21). *Understand your world with Bing.* Microsoft Bing Blogs. https://blogs.bing.com /search/2013/03/21/understand-your-world-with-bing/

Quine, W. V. O. (1948/2011). On what there is. In R. B. Talisse & S. F. Aikin (Eds.), *The pragmatism reader: From Peirce through the present* (pp. 221–33). Princeton University Press.

Radford, A., Wu, J., Child, R., Luan, D., Amodei, D., & Sutskever, I. (2019). *Language models are unsupervised multitask learners.* OpenAI blog. https://openai.com /blog/better-language-models/

Raffel, C., Shazeer, N., Roberts, A., Lee, K., Narang, S.,

Matena, M., ... Liu, P. J. (2019). Exploring the limits of transfer learning with a unified text-to-text transformer. https://arxiv.org/abs/1910.10683

Raghavan, P. (2020, October 15). *How AI is powering a more helpful Google.* Google Blog. https://blog.google/products/search/search-on/

Raman, T. V. (2018, July 24). *Hey Google, what's the latest news?* Google Search Central Blog. https://developers.google.com/search/blog/2018/07/hey-google-whats-latest-news

Rastogi, A., Zang, X., Sunkara, S., Gupta, R., & Khaitan, P. (2020). Towards scalable multi-domain conversational agents: The schema-guided dialogue dataset. *Proceedings of the AAAI Conference on Artificial Intelligence, 34*(5), 8689–96.

Ray, L. (2020, March 2). *2020 Google search survey: How much do users trust their search results?* Moz. https://moz.com/blog/2020-google-search-survey

Reagle, J. (1999, December 10). *Eskimo snow and Scottish rain: Legal considerations of schema design.* W3C. https://www.w3.org/TR/md-policy-design

Reagle, J. & Koerner, J. (Eds.). (2020). *Wikipedia @ 20: Stories of an incomplete revolution.* MIT Press.

Recollet, K., & Johnson, J. (2019). "Why do you need to know that?" Slipstream movements and mapping "Otherwise" in Tkaronto. *Journal of Public Pedagogies,* (4). https://doi.org/10.15209/jpp.1187

Redi, M., Gerlach, M., Johnson, I., Morgan, J., & Zia, L. (2020). A taxonomy of knowledge gaps for Wikimedia projects. https://arxiv.org/abs/2008.12314

Ribes, D., Hoffman, A. S., Slota, S. C., & Bowker, G. C. (2019). The logic of domains. *Social Studies of Science, 49*(3), 281–309. https://doi.org/10.1177/0306312719849709

Rieder, B. (2005). Networked control: Search engines and the symmetry of confidence. *The International Review of Information Ethics, 3,* 26–32. https://doi.org/10.29173/irie346

Rieder, B. (2009). Democratizing search? From critique to society-oriented design. In K. Becker & F. Stalder (Eds.), *Deep search: The politics of search beyond Google* (pp. 133–51). StudienVerlag.

Rieder, B., & Sire, G. (2014). Conflicts of interest and incentives to bias: A microeconomic critique of Google's tangled position on the Web. *New Media & Society, 16*(2), 195–211. https://doi.org/10.1177/1461444813481195

Riemer, N. (2010). *Introducing semantics.* Cambridge University Press.

Roberts, S. T. (2019). *Behind the screen: Content moderation in the shadows of social media.* Yale University Press.

Roser, M., Ritchie, H., & Ortiz-Ospina, E. (2015). *Internet.* Our World in Data. https://ourworldindata.org/internet

Safavi, T., & Koutra, D. (2021). Relational world knowledge representation in contextual language models: A review. https://arxiv.org/abs/2104.05837

Sankar, S., Lassen, S., & Curtiss, M. (2013, March 6). *Under the hood: Building out the infrastructure for graph search.* Engineering at Meta. https://engineering.fb.com/2013/03/06/core-data/under-the-hood-building-out-the-infrastructure-for-graph-search/

Schreiber, G., & Raimond, Y. (2014, June 24). *RDF 1.1 Primer.* W3C. https://www.w3.org/TR/rdf11-primer/

Schwartz, B. (2014, March 12). *Google to publishers concerned over the Knowledge Graph; Searchers still need your content.* Search Engine Land. https://searchengineland.com/google-publishers-concerned-knowledge-graph-searchers-still-need-content-186325

Sculley, D., Holt, G., Golovin, D., Davydov, E., Phillips, T., Ebner, D., ... Dennison, D. (2015). Hidden technical debt in machine learning systems. *Proceedings of the 28th international conference on Neural information processing systems, Vol. 2 (NIPS '15)* (pp. 2503–11).

Sequeda, J. F., & Lassila, O. (2021). *Designing and*

building enterprise knowledge graphs. Morgan & Claypool.

Shaban, H. (2018, March 20). Google announces plan to combat spread of misinformation. *Washington Post.* https://www.washingtonpost.com/news/the-switch/wp /2018/03/20/google-announces-plan-to-combat-spread -of-misinformation

Shannon, C. E. (1948). A mathematical theory of communication. *The Bell System Technical Journal, 27*(3), 379–423.

Sharma, S. (2014). *In the meantime: Temporality and cultural politics.* Duke University Press.

Shaw, R. (2015). Big Data and reality. *Big Data & Society, 2*(2). https://doi.org/10.1177/2053951715608877

Sheth, A., Avant, D., & Bertram, C. (2001). *System and method for creating a semantic web and its applications in browsing, searching, profiling, personalization and advertising* (US6311194B1). https://patents.google.com /patent/US6311194B1/en

Simonite, T. (2019, February 18). *Inside the Alexa-friendly world of Wikidata.* Wired. https://www.wired.com /story/inside-the-alexa-friendly-world-of-wikidata/

Singhal, A. (2012, May 16). *Introducing the Knowledge Graph: Things, not strings.* Google Blog. https://blog .google/products/search/introducing-knowledge-graph -things-not/

Slawski, B. (2013a, May 9). *How Google decides what to know in a knowledge panel.* SEO by the Sea. https:// www.seobythesea.com/2013/05/google-knowledge -graph-results/

Slawski, B. (2013b, September 23). *The Google Hummingbird update and the likely patent behind Hummingbird.* SEO by the Sea. https://www.seobythesea .com/2013/09/google-hummingbird-patent/

Slawski, B. (2014, September 4). *Google's browseable fact repository – an early knowledge graph.* SEO by the Sea. https://www.seobythesea.com/2014/09/googles -browseable-fact-repository-early-knowledge-graph/

Slawski, B. (2018a, June 22). *Five years of Google ranking signals*. SEO by the Sea. https://www.seobythesea.com /2018/06/google-ranking-signals/#a200

Slawski, B. (2018b, November 28). *How Google might predict query intent using contextual histories*. Go Fish Digital. https://gofishdigital.com/query-intent -contextual-histories/

Slawski, B. (2019a, July 10). *How Google may handle question answering when facts are missing*. SEO by the Sea. https://www.seobythesea.com/2019/07/how -google-may-handle-question-answering-when-facts-are -missing/

Slawski, B. (2019b, July 17). *How would Google answer vague questions in queries?* SEO by the Sea. https:// www.seobythesea.com/2019/07/how-would-google -answer-vague-questions-in-queries/

Slawski, B. (2020, June 29). *Ranked entities in search results at Google*. Search Engine Journal. https://www .searchenginejournal.com/ranked-entities-google-search -results/372973/#close

Smith, B. (2004). Ontology. In L. Floridi (Ed.), *The Blackwell guide to the philosophy of computing and information* (pp. 155–66). Blackwell.

Smythe, D. W. (1977). Communications: Blindspot of Western Marxism. *Canadian Journal of Political and Social Theory*, 1(3), 1–27. https://journals.uvic.ca/index .php/ctheory/article/view/13715

Sowa, J. F. (1976). Conceptual graphs for a data base interface. *IBM Journal of Research and Development*, 20(4), 336–57. https://doi.org/10.1147/rd.204.0336

Sowa, J. F. (1984). *Conceptual structures: Information processing in mind and machine*. Addison-Wesley.

Sowa, J. F. (1999). *Knowledge representation: Logical, philosophical, and computational foundations*. Brooks/ Cole.

Spink, A., & Zimmer, M. (Eds.). (2008). *Web search: Multidisciplinary perspectives*. Springer.

Spivack, N. (2010, January 26). *How Siri works – interview with Tom Gruber, CTO of Siri.* Nova Spivack. http://www.novaspivack.com/technology/how-hisiri-works-interview-with-tom-gruber-cto-of-siri

Stallman, R. (2002). *Free software, free society: Selected essays of Richard M. Stallman.* GNU Press. https://www.gnu.org/philosophy/fsfs/rms-essays.pdf

Steiner, T., Troncy, R., & Hausenblas, M. (2010). How Google is using linked data today and vision for tomorrow. *Proceedings of Linked Data in the Future Internet at the Future Internet Assembly (FIA 2010), Ghent, December 2010.* https://research.google/pubs/pub37430/

Stocky, T., & Rasmussen, L. (2013, January 15). *Introducing Graph Search Beta.* Meta. https://about.fb.com/news/2013/01/introducing-graph-search-beta/

Suchanek, F., Kasneci, G., & Weikum, G. (2007). Yago: A core of semantic knowledge. In *WWW '07: Proceedings of the 16th international conference on World Wide Web* (pp. 697–706). ACM. https://doi.org/10.1145/1242572.1242667

Sullivan, D. (2020, May 20). *A reintroduction to our Knowledge Graph and knowledge panels.* Google Blog. https://blog.google/products/search/about-knowledge-graph-and-knowledge-panels/

Sullivan, D. (2021, March 24). *Google Search sends more traffic to the open web every year.* Google. https://blog.google/products/search/google-search-sends-more-traffic-open-web-every-year/

Sun, E. (2013). *Under the hood: The Entities Graph.* Facebook. https://m.facebook.com/nt/screen/?params=%7B%22note_id%22%3A10158791581767200%7D&path=%2Fnotes%2Fnote%2F&_rdr=&s=09

Sun, J., & Peng, N. (2021). Men are elected, women are married: Events gender bias on Wikipedia. https://arxiv.org/abs/2106.01601

Sundin, O., Haider, J., Andersson, C., Carlsson, H., & Kjellberg, S. (2017). The search-ification of everyday life and the mundane-ification of search. *Journal of*

Documentation, 73(2), 224–43. https://doi.org/10.1108 /JD-06-2016-0081

Sundin, O., Lewandowski, D., & Haider, J. (2022). Whose relevance? Web search engines as multisided relevance machines. *Journal of the Association for Information Science and Technology*, 73(5), 637–42. https://doi.org /10.1002/ASI.24570

Sweeney, M. E. (2016a). The intersectional interface. In S. U. Noble & B. M. Tynes (Eds.), *The intersectional internet: Race, sex, class, and culture online* (pp. 215–28). Peter Lang.

Sweeney, M. E. (2016b). The Ms. Dewey "experience:" Technoculture, gender, and race. In J. Daniels, K. Gregory, & T. McMillian Cottom (Eds.), *Digital sociologies* (pp. 401–20). Policy Press.

Szeredi, P., Lukácsy, G., & Benkő, T. (2014). *The semantic web explained: The technology and mathematics behind web 3.0*. Cambridge University Press.

Target, S. (2018, May 27). *Whatever happened to the Semantic Web?* Two-Bit History. https://twobithistory .org/2018/05/27/semantic-web.html

Tharani, K. (2021). Much more than a mere technology: A systematic review of Wikidata in libraries. *The Journal of Academic Librarianship*, 47(2). 102326. https://doi .org/10.1016/j.acalib.2021.102326

Thomas, N. (2018). *Becoming-social in a networked age*. Routledge.

Thomer, A. K., & Wickett, K. M. (2020). Relational data paradigms: What do we learn by taking the materiality of databases seriously? *Big Data & Society*, 7(1). https://doi.org/10.1177/2053951720934838

Thornton, P. (2017, November 28). *Geographies of (con)text: language and structure in a digital age*. Computational Culture. http://computationalculture.net/geographies-of -context-language-and-structure-in-a-digital-age/

Thornton, P. (2018). A critique of linguistic capitalism: Provocation/intervention. *GeoHumanities*, 4(2), 417–37. https://doi.org/10.1080/2373566X.2018.1486724

Tkacz, N. (2014). *Wikipedia and the politics of openness.* University of Chicago Press.

Tripodi, F. (2021). Ms. Categorized: Gender, notability, and inequality on Wikipedia: *New Media & Society.* https://doi.org/10.1177/14614448211023772

Turki, H., Hadj Taieb, M. A., Shafee, T., Lubiana, T., Jemielniak, D., Aouicha, M. B., ... & Mietchen, D. (2022). Representing COVID-19 information in collaborative knowledge graphs: The case of Wikidata. *Semantic Web*, *13*(2), 233–64. https://content.iospress .com/articles/semantic-web/sw210444

Uyar, A. & Aliyu, F. (2015). Evaluating search features of Google Knowledge Graph and Bing Satori. *Online Information Review*, *39*, 197–213. https://doi.org/10 .1108/OIR-10-2014-0257

Vaidhyanathan, S. (2011). *The Googlization of everything: (And why we should worry).* University of California Press.

Vaidhyanathan, S. (2018). *Antisocial media: How Facebook disconnects us and undermines democracy.* Oxford University Press.

van Couvering, E. (2008). The history of the Internet search engine: Navigational media and the traffic commodity. In A. Spink & M. Zimmer (Eds.), *Web search: Multidisciplinary perspectives* (pp. 177–206). Springer. https://doi.org/10.1007/978-3-540-75829 -7_11

van Dijck, J., & Poell, T. (2013). Understanding social media logic. *Media and Communication*, *1*(1), 2–14. https://doi.org/10.17645/mac.v1i1.70

van Dijck, J., Poell, T., & de Waal, M. (2018). *The platform society: Public values in a connective world.* Oxford University Press.

Vandenbussche, P.-Y., Atemezing, G. A., Poveda-Villalón, M., & Vatant, B. (2017). Linked Open Vocabularies (LOV): A gateway to reusable semantic vocabularies on the Web. *Semantic Web Journal*, *8*(3), 437–52. https:// content.iospress.com/articles/semantic-web/sw213

Vang, K. J. (2013). Ethics of Google's Knowledge Graph: Some considerations. *Journal of Information, Communication and Ethics in Society, 11*(4), 245–60. https://www.emerald.com/insight/content/doi/10.1108 /JICES-08-2013-0028/full/html

Velikovich, L., Williams, I., Scheiner, J., Aleksic, P. S., Moreno, P. J., & Riley, M. (2018). Semantic lattice processing in contextual automatic speech recognition for Google Assistant. In *Interspeech 2018* (pp. 2222–6). International Speech Communication Association.

Vlahos, J. (2019). *Talk to me: How voice computing will transform the way we live, work, and think.* Houghton Mifflin Harcourt.

Vrana, A., Sengupta, A., Pozo, C., & Bouterse, S. (2020). *Decolonizing the internet's languages – Summary report.* Whose Knowledge? https://whoseknowledge.org /resource/dtil-report/

Vrandečić, D. (2012). Wikidata: A new platform for collaborative data collection. In *WWW '12 Companion: Proceedings of the 21st International Conference on World Wide Web* (pp. 1063–4). https://doi.org/10.1145 /2187980.2188242

Vrandečić, D. (2020). Collaborating on the sum of all knowledge across languages. In J. Reagle & J. Koerner (Eds.), *Wikipedia @ 20: Stories of an incomplete revolution* (pp. 175–88). MIT Press.

Vrandečić, D., & Krötzsch, M. (2014). Wikidata: A free collaborative knowledgebase. *Communications of the ACM, 57*(10), 78–85. https://doi.org/10.1145/2629489

Wallace, J. (2018). Modelling contemporary gatekeeping: The rise of individuals, algorithms and platforms in digital news dissemination. *Digital Journalism, 6*(3), 274–93. https://doi.org/10.1080/21670811.2017 .1343648

Waller, V. (2016). Making knowledge machine-processable: Some implications of general semantic search. *Behaviour & Information Technology, 35*(10), 784–95. https://doi .org/10.1080/0144929X.2016.1183710

Wei, X., & Liao, Y. (2019, January 29). *Contextualizing Airbnb by building knowledge graph*. Airbnb Tech Blog. https://medium.com/@xiaoya2wei

West, R., Gabrilovich, E., Murphy, K., Sun, S., Gupta, R., & Lin, D. (2014). Knowledge base completion via search-based question answering. In *WWW '14: Proceedings of the 23rd international conference on world wide web* (pp. 515–26). https://doi.org/10.1145 /2566486.2568032

Wheaton, K. (2018). *Ask a researcher: What does "best" really mean?* Think with Google. https://www .thinkwithgoogle.com/marketing-strategies/search/best -searches/

Whose Knowledge? (2022). *Decolonizing the Internet's structured data*. Whose Knowledge? https://whoseknowledge .org/resource/dti-structured-data-report/

Wiggers, K. (2019, November 1). *Amazon is poorly vetting Alexa's user-submitted answers*. Venture Beat. https://venturebeat.com/2019/11/01/amazon-alexa -answers-vetting-user-questions

Wihbey, J. P. (2019). *The social fact: News and knowledge in a networked world*. MIT Press.

Wilson, K. (2020, November 2). *The world's second largest Wikipedia is written almost entirely by one bot*. Vice. https://www.vice.com/en/article/4agamm /the-worlds-second-largest-wikipedia-is-written-almost -entirely-by-one-bot

Winseck, D. (2017). The geopolitical economy of the global internet infrastructure. *Journal of Information Policy, 7*, 228–267. https://doi.org/10.5325/JINFOPOLI .7.2017.0228

Wittgenstein, L. (1953). *Philosophical Investigations* (trans. G. E. M. Anscombe). Basil Blackwell.

Woods, W. A. (1975). What's in a link: Foundations for semantic networks. In D. G. Bobrow & A. Collins (Eds.), *Representation and Understanding* (pp. 35–82). Morgan Kaufmann. https://doi.org/10.1016/B978-0-12 -108550-6.50007-0

Yasunaga, M., Ren, H., Bosselut, A., Liang, P., & Leskovec, J. (2021). QA-GNN: Reasoning with language models and knowledge graphs for question answering. https://arxiv.org/abs/2104.06378

Zeng, M. L., & Qin, J. (2016). *Metadata* (2nd ed.). Neal Schuman.

Zimmer, M. (2010). Web search studies: Multidisciplinary perspectives on web search engines. In J. Hunsinger, L. Klastrup, & M. Allen (Eds.), *International handbook of internet research* (pp. 507–21). Springer.

Zverina, J. (2020, June 1). Fighting COVID-19 with knowledge graphs. *UC San Diego News Center*. https://ucsdnews.ucsd.edu/pressrelease/fighting-covid-19-with-knowledge-graphs

Index